## Third Edition

# CIRCLES OF LEARNING:

## Cooperation in the Classroom

David W. Johnson,

Roger T. Johnson,

and

Edythe Johnson Holubec

Published by
Interaction Book Company
7208 Cornelia Drive
Edina, Minnesota 55435
(612) 831-9500

Johnson, Johnson, & Holubec

Library of Congress Card Catalog Number: 86-081701

ISBN 0-939603-12-8

Printing (Last Digit)

10 9 8 7 6 5 4 3 2

## Dedication

This book is dedicated to our parents, Roger and Frances Johnson who discouraged inappropriate competition and taught us to cooperate

## Acknowledgments

Thanks are due to the thousands of teachers who have taken their training in structuring cooperative learning groups back into the classroom and created an environment where students care about each other and each other's learning. They have taught us a lot over the years. A special thanks to Judy Bartlett, our office manager at the Cooperative Learning Center, who deals with people with charm and patience, and an even more difficult task, deals with us with charm and patience. She went far beyond the call of duty (as she always does) to get this book in print.

# Table Of Contents

**Chapter**                                                    **Page**

# Chapter One

# What Is Cooperative Learning?

## Introduction

On July 15, 1982, Don Bennett, a Seattle businessman, was the first amputee ever to climb Mount Rainier (reported in Kouzes & Posner, 1987). He climbed 14,410 feet on one leg and two crutches. It took him five days. When asked to state the most important lesson he learned from doing so, without hesitation he said, "You can't do it alone."

In every classroom, no matter what the subject area or age of the students, teachers may structure lessons so that students:

1. Work collaboratively in small groups, ensuring that all members master the assigned material.

2. Engage in a win-lose struggle to see who is best.

3. Work independently on their own learning goals at their own pace and in their own space to achieve a preset criterion of excellence.

We are currently leaving an era of competitive and individualistic learning. The "me" classrooms and "do your own thing" seatwork are fading. We are entering an era of interdependence and mutuality in schools. **The current trend is for "we" classrooms and "we are all in this together" learning.** In contrast to fads, which are generated from the top down, trends are generated from the bottom up and, like horses, they are easier to ride in the direction they are already going. This book is about the trend, being set by teachers and administrators from all parts of our country, toward utilizing cooperative learning procedures in classrooms from preschools to graduate schools.

After half a century of relative neglect, cooperative learning procedures are increasingly being used throughout public and private schools and colleges. The intent of this book is to provide teachers with the knowledge required for beginning the journey of gaining expertise in using cooperative learning. In order to do so, teachers must:

1. Conceptually understand what cooperative learning is and how it differs from competitive and individualistic learning (Chapter 1).

2. Conceptually understand the essential components that differentiate cooperative learning from "traditional classroom grouping" and "individualistic efforts with talking" (Chapter 1). Two of the most important and complex components are positive interdependence and the teaching of social skills (Chapters 4 and 5).

3. Conceptually understand the teacher's role in using cooperative learning (Chapter 3).

4. Be able to plan and teach cooperative lessons.

5. Be personally committed to gaining expertise in using cooperative learning. This commitment must be rationale in the sense that it is built on knowledge of the theory and research supporting the use of cooperative learning (Chapter 2).

6. Be part of a colleagial support group made up of teachers who are working hard to gain expertise in the use of cooperative learning within their classrooms (Chapter 7).

# Student-Student Interaction

Jim is sitting in the classroom, doing nothing. His book is open-- to the wrong page. His sheet of printed questions has disappeared. He does not care. He is 17 years old. His classmates ignore him. Within a competitive class Jim is considered a loser to be shunned. Within an individualistic class Jim is considered irrelevant to one's own striving for personal success.

When students are required to **compete** with each other for grades, they work against each other to achieve a goal that only one or a few students can attain. Students are graded on a norm-referenced basis, which requires them to work faster and more accurately than their peers. In doing so, they strive to be better than classmates ("Who can beat Jim in math?"), work to deprive others ("You win, Jim loses."), to celebrate classmates' failures ("Jim did not do his homework, that puts you ahead."), view resources such as grades as limited ("Remember, in a class of 30, only 5 people can get an A."), recognize their negatively linked fate (the more you gain, the less for me; the more I gain, the less for you), and believe that the more competent and hard working individuals become "haves" and the less competent and deserving individuals become the "have nots" (only the strong prosper). In **competitive situations** there is a negative inter-dependence among goal achievements; students perceive that they can obtain their goals if and only if the other students in the class fail to obtain their goals (Deutsch, 1962; Johnson & Johnson, 1987). Unfortunately, most students perceive school as predominantly a competitive enterprise. They either work hard in school to do better than the other students, or they take it easy because they do not believe they have a chance to win.

When students are required to work **individualistically** on their own, they work by themselves to accomplish learning goals unrelated to those of the other students. Individual goals are assigned each day, students' efforts are evaluated on a criteria-referenced basis. Each student has his or her own set of materials and works at his or her own speed, ignoring the other students in the class. Students are expected and encouraged to focus on their strict self-interest ("How well can I do?"), valuing only their own efforts and own success ("If I study hard, I may get a high grade."), and ignoring as irrelevant the success or failure of others ("Whether Jim studies or not does not affect me"). In **individualistic learning situations**, students' goal achievements are independent; students perceive that the achievement of their learning goals is unrelated to what other students do (Deutsch, 1962; Johnson & Johnson, 1987).

Consider again the case of Jim, who is sitting in the classroom doing nothing. The teacher assigns all students to cooperative learning groups. Jim finds himself sitting with three class mates. "Jim, where is your paper?" they immediately ask. "Don't know," Jim replied. "Here are the questions," the group members reply, "let's go over them and make sure you know the answers. Don't worry. We'll help you." **Cooperation** is working together to accomplish shared goals. Within cooperative activities individuals seek outcomes that are beneficial to themselves **and** beneficial to all other group members. **Cooperative learning** is the instructional use of small groups so that students work together to maximize their own and each other's learning. The idea is simple. Class members are split into groups of from two to five members after receiving instruction from the teacher. They then work through the assignment until all group members have successfully understood and completed it. Cooperative efforts result in participants striving for mutual benefit so that all group members benefit from one's efforts ("Jim, your success benefits me and my success benefits you."), recognizing that all group members share a common fate ("We all sink or swim together here."), recognizing that one's performance is mutually caused by oneself and one's colleagues ("We can not do it without you, Jim."), and feeling proud and jointly celebrating when a group member is recognized for achievement ("Jim, you got an B! That is terrific!"). In cooperative learning situations there is a positive interdependence among students' goal attainments; students perceive that they can reach their learning goals if and only if the other students in the learning group also reach their goals (Deutsch, 1962; Johnson & Johnson, 1987).

In summary, students' learning goals may be structured to promote cooperative, competitive, or no interdependence among students as they strive to accomplish their learning goals. In every classroom, instructional activities are aimed at accomplishing goals and are conducted under a goal structure. A **learning goal** is a desired future state of demonstrating competence or mastery in the subject area being studied, such as conceptual understanding of math processes, facility in the proper use of a language, or mastering the procedures of inquiry. The **goal structure** specifies the ways in which students will interact with each other and the teacher during the instructional session. Each goal structure has its place. In the ideal classroom, all students would learn how to work collaboratively with others, compete for fun and enjoyment, and work autonomously on their own. The teacher decides which goal structure to implement within each lesson. If cooperation is the only way students learn in school, they may never learn to compete appropriately for fun or have the opportunity to follow a learning trail on their own (Johnson & Johnson, 1987, 1988). Thus, competitive and individualistic work should supplement cooperative learning when it is appropriate.

Cooperative learning is the most important of the three types of learning situations, yet currently it is the least used. Current evidence indicates that class sessions are structured cooperatively only for 7 to 20 percent of the time (Anderson, 1984; Goodlad, 1983; D. Johnson & Johnson, 1976; R. Johnson, 1976; R. Johnson, Johnson, & Bryant, 1973; Schumaker, Sheldon-Wildgen, & Sherman, 1980). On the other hand, what we know about effective instruction indicates that cooperative learning should be used when we want students to learn more, like school better, like each other better, like themselves better, and learn more effective social skills. It is clear from the research that classrooms should be dominated by cooperation among students. In the next sections of this chapter, therefore, we shall give a brief history of cooperative learning, define its essential components, and note the differences between cooperative learning and traditional small group instruction.

# History Of Cooperative Learning

*"Two are better than one, because they have a good reward for their toil. For if they fall, one will lift up his fellow; but woe to him who is alone when he falls and has not another to lift him up...And though a man might prevail against one who is alone, two will withstand him. A threefold cord is not quickly broken."*

Ecclesiastics 4:9-12

**Cooperative learning is an old idea.** The capacity to work cooperatively has been a major contributor to the survival of our species. The Talmud clearly states that in order to learn one must have a learning partner. As early as the first century, Quintilian argued that students could benefit from teaching one another. **Johann Amos Comenius** (1592-1679) believed that students would benefit both by teaching and being taught by other students. In the late 1700's **Joseph Lancaster** and Andrew Bell made extensive use of cooperative learning groups in England, and the idea was brought to America when a Lancastrian school was opened in New York City in 1806. Within the **Common School Movement** in the United States in the early 1800's there was a strong emphasis on cooperative learning. Certainly, the use of cooperative learning is not new to American education. There have been periods in which cooperative learning had strong advocates and was widely used to promote the educational goals of that time.

One of the most successful advocates of cooperative learning was **Colonel Francis Parker**. In the last three decades of the 19th Century, Colonel Parker brought to his advocacy of cooperative learning enthusiasm, idealism, practicality, and an intense devotion to freedom, democracy, and individuality in the public schools. His fame and success rested on the vivid and regenerating spirit that he brought into the schoolroom and on his power to create a classroom atmosphere that was truly cooperative and democratic. When he was superintendent of the public schools at Quincy, Massachusetts (1875-1880), he averaged more than 30,000 visitors a year to examine his use of cooperative learning procedures. Parker's instructional methods of promoting cooperation among students dominated American education through the turn of the century. Following Parker, **John Dewey** promoted the use of cooperative learning groups as part of his famous project method in instruction. In the late 1930's, however, interpersonal competition began to be emphasized in public schools.

In the 1940's **Morton Deutsch**, building on the theorizing of **Kurt Lewin**, proposed a theory of cooperative and competitive situations that has served as the primary foundation on which subsequent research on and discussion of cooperative learning has been based. Our own research is directly based on Deutsch's work. There are several groups of researchers and practitioners scattered throughout the United States and Canada and in several other countries engaged in the study and implementation of cooperative learning lessons, curriculums, strategies, and procedures.

William Glasser, the author of **Schools Without Failure** and **Control Theory**, has recently published a new book on classroom practices entitled **Control Theory in the Classroom**. In this practical and useful book he describes how teachers may use control theory and cooperative learning to ensure that students (1) feel like they are involved in relationships with peers who care about and assist each other, (2) are able to influence the people they are involved with, and (3) enjoy learning. It is through belonging, power, and fun that students are motivated to work up to their potential and to maintain interest in learning.

# Not All Group Learning Is Cooperative Learning

In a classroom the teacher is trying out learning groups. "This is a mess," she thinks. In one group students are bickering over who is going to do the writing. In another group a member sits quietly, too shy to participate. Two members of a third group are

7

talking about football while the third member works on the assignment. "My students do not know how to work cooperatively," the teacher concludes.

What is a teacher to do in such a situation? Simply placing students in groups and telling them to work together does not mean that they know how to cooperate or that they will do so even if they know. Sitting students near each other and telling them that they are a group in and of itself does not produce cooperation or the higher achievement and other outcomes typically found in cooperative learning groups.

There are many ways in which the efforts of **traditional learning groups** may go wrong. Group members sometimes seek a free ride on others' work by "leaving it to Roger" to complete the group's tasks. Students who are stuck with doing all the work sometimes decrease their efforts to avoid being suckers. High ability group members may take over the important leadership roles in ways that benefit themselves at the expense of the lower achieving group members so that the rich-get-richer. In a traditional learning group, for example, the more able group member may give all the explanations of what is being learned. Since the amount of time spent explaining correlates highly with the amount learned, the more able member learns a great deal while the less able members flounder as a captive audience. Group work may break down because of divisive conflicts and power struggles. Dysfunctional divisions of labor may be formulated ("I'm the thinkist and you're the typist"). Inappropriate dependence on authority may exist. Group members may gang up against a task. Pressures to conform may suppress individual efforts. There are multiple ways that groups may fail.

The barriers to effective group learning are avoided when it is properly structured cooperatively. Effective cooperative learning occurs when you ensure that the essential components are structured within each cooperative lesson.

# Essential Components of Cooperative Learning

In Roy Smith's Junior High School English class in Hingham, Massachusetts, students are given the assignment of writing thesis essays on a story, **The Choice**, which discusses the experience of a time traveler who goes into the future and returns. The class is divided into groups of four, with high-, medium-, and low-achieving students and both male and female students in each group. Seven instructional tasks are assigned over a four day unit:

1. A prereading discussion on what should be taken on a time- travel trip into the future, what should be found out, and what should be told to others on one's return.

2. Each student writes a letter/proposal requesting funding for a time-travel into the future.

3. Group members edit each other's letters/proposals and gives suggestions for improvement and mark any errors that need correcting. All revised letters/proposals are handed in with the signatures of the group members who edited them.

4. Each member reads the story, **The Choice**, and makes a tentative interpretation of its meaning.

5. Group members discuss the story and reach consensus on the answers to seven questions about its content.

6. Each student writes a composition, taking the position that the decision made by Williams was correct or incorrect and presenting a convincing rationale as to why his or her position is valid.

7. Group members edit two other members' compositions. Careful editing for spelling, punctuation, and the components of thesis essays is emphasized. All revised com-

positions are handed in with the signatures of the group members who edited them.

Within this lesson **positive interdependence** is structured by having each group start out with 100 points, and subtracting 5 points for every spelling or punctuation error and every failure to include the essential components of thesis essays. The group is given 20 bonus points if every member clearly articulates an interpretation of the story and supports it with valid reasoning. **Individual accountability** is ensured by requiring each student to write the letter/proposal and essay and revise them to meet the standards of his or her groupmates. The **cooperative skill** of criticizing ideas without criticizing the person is explained by the teacher and practiced by the students. Finally, the group spends some time during the final class session **processing** how well they worked together and what they could do in the future to be an even more effective group member. This lesson illustrates the essential components of cooperative learning.

Many educators who believe that they are using cooperative learning are, in fact, missing its essence. There is a crucial difference between simply putting students into groups to learn and in structuring cooperation among students.

Cooperation is **not** having students sit side-by-side at the same table to talk with each other as they do their individual assignments. Cooperation is **not** assigning a report to a group of students where one student does all the work and the others put their names on the product as well. Cooperation is much more than being physically near other students, discussing material with other students, helping other students, or sharing material among students, although each of these is important in cooperative learning. There are five essential components that must be included for small group learning to be truly cooperative.

## Positive Interdependence

*"All for one and one for all."*

Alexandre Dumas

Within a football game, the quarterback who throws the pass and the receiver who catches the pass are positively interdependent. The success of one depends on the success of the other. It takes two to complete a pass. One player cannot succeed without the other. Both have to perform competently if their mutual success is to be assured. They sink or swim together.

The first requirement for an effectively structured cooperative lesson is that students believe that they "sink or swim together." Within cooperative learning situations students have two responsibilities: learn the assigned material and ensure that all members of their group learn the assigned material. The technical term for that dual responsibility is positive interdependence. **Positive interdependence** exists when students perceive that they are linked with groupmates in a way so that they cannot succeed unless their groupmates do (and vice versa) and/or that they must coordinate their efforts with the efforts of their groupmates to complete a task. Positive interdependence promotes a situation in which students see that their work benefits groupmates and vice versa, and students work together in small groups to maximize the learning of all members by sharing their resources, providing mutual support, and celebrating their joint success.

When positive interdependence is clearly understood, it highlights:

1. Each group member's efforts are required and indispensable for group success (i.e., there can be no "free-riders").

2. Each group member has a unique contribution to make to the joint effort because of his or her resources and/or role and task responsibilities.

There are a number of ways of structuring positive interdependence within a learning group (goal, reward, resource, and role interdependence). To ensure that students believe "they sink or swim together" and care about how much each other learns, you (the teacher) have to structure a clear **group or mutual goal** such as "learn the assigned material and make sure that all members of your group learn the assigned material." The group goal always has to be part of the lesson. To supplement goal interdependence, you may wish to add **joint rewards** (if all members of the group score 90 percent correct or better on the test, each will receive 5 bonus points), **divided resources** (giving each group member a part of the total information required to complete an assignment), and **complementary roles** (reader, checker, encourager, elaborator).

## Face-To-Face Promotive Interaction

> *"In an industrial organization it's group effort that counts. There's really no room for stars in an industrial organization. You need talented people, but they can't do it alone. They have to have help."*

John F. Donnelly, President, Donnelly Mirrors

The second component is **face-to-face promotive interaction** among group members. Cooperative learning requires face-to-face interaction among students within which they promote each other's learning and success. There is no magic in positive interdependence in and of itself. It is the interaction patterns and verbal interchange among students promoted by the positive interdependence that affect education outcomes.

Within cooperative lessons, you need to maximize the opportunity for students to promote each other's success by helping, assisting, supporting, encouraging, and praising each other's efforts to learn. Such promotive interaction has a number of effects. **First**, there are cognitive activities and interpersonal dynamics that only occur when students explain to each other how the answers to assignments are derived. This includes orally explaining how to solve problems, discussing the nature of the concepts being learned, teaching one's knowledge to groupmates, and explaining how present learning is connected with past learning. **Second**, it is within face-to-face interaction that the opportunity for a wide variety of social influences and patterns emerge. Helping and assisting take place. Accountability to peers, influencing each other's reasoning and conclusions, social modeling, social support, and interpersonal rewards all increase as the face-to-face interaction among group members increase. **Third**, the verbal and nonverbal responses of other group members provide important feedback concerning each other's performance. **Fourth**, it provides an opportunity for peers to pressure unmotivated group members to achieve. **Fifth**, it is the interaction involved in completing the work that allows students to get to know each other as persons, which in turn forms the basis for caring and committed relationships among members.

To obtain meaningful face-to-face interaction, the size of groups needs to be small (from 2 to 6 members), as the perception that one's participation and efforts are needed increases as the size of the group decreases. On the other hand, as the size of the group increases the amount of pressure peers may place on unmotivated group members increases. Whatever the size, the effects of social interaction cannot be achieved through nonsocial substitutes such as instructions and materials.

## Individual Accountability / Personal Responsibility

> *"What children can do together today, they can do alone tomorrow."*

> Vygotsky

Among the early settlers of Massachusetts there was a saying, "If you do not work, you do not eat." The third essential component of cooperative learning is **individual accountability**, which exists when the performance of each individual student is assessed and the results given back to the group and the individual. It is important that the group knows who needs more assistance, support, and encouragement in completing the assignment. It is also important that group members know that they cannot "hitch-hike" on the work of others.

To ensure that each student is individually accountable to do his or her fair share of the group's work, you need to:

1. Assess how much effort each member is contributing to the group's work.

2. Provide feedback to groups and individual students.

3. Help groups avoid redundant efforts by members.

4. Ensure that every member is responsible for the final outcome.

When it is difficult to identify members' contributions, when members' contributions are redundant, and when members are not responsible for the final group outcome, members are likely to loaf and seek a free ride. The smaller the size of the group, furthermore, the greater the individual accountability may be.

**The purpose of cooperative learning groups is to make each member a stronger individual.** Individual accountability is the key to ensuring that all group members are in fact strengthened by learning cooperatively. After participating in a cooperative lesson, group members should be better able to complete similar tasks by themselves. There is a pattern to classroom learning. First, students learn how to solve the problem or use the strategy in a cooperative group, then secondly, they perform it alone. Common ways to structure individual accountability include giving an individual test to each student, randomly selecting one student's product to represent the entire group, having students teach what they have learned to someone else, and have students explain what they know to the group.

## Interpersonal And Small Group Skills

*"I will pay more for the ability to deal with people than any other ability under the sun."*

John D. Rockefeller

The fourth essential component of cooperative learning is the appropriate use of **interpersonal and small group skills**. Placing socially unskilled individuals in a group and telling them to cooperate does not guarantee that they are able to do so effectively. We are not born instinctively knowing how to interact effectively with others. Interpersonal and group skills do not magically appear when they are needed. Persons must be taught the social skills required for high quality collaboration and be motivated to use them if cooperative groups are to be productive. In order to coordinate efforts to achieve mutual goals, students must (1) get to know and trust each other, (2) communicate accurately and unambiguously, (3) accept and support each other, and (4) resolve conflicts constructively (Johnson, 1986, 1987; Johnson & F. Johnson, 1987). Interpersonal and small group skills form the basic nexus among students, and if students are to work together productively and cope with the stresses and strains of doing so, they must have a modicum of these skills.

## Group Processing

The fifth essential component of cooperative learning is **group processing**, which exists when group members discuss how well they are achieving their goals and maintaining effective working relationships. Effective group work is influenced by whether or not groups reflect on (i.e., process) how well they are functioning. A **process** is an identifiable sequence of events taking place over time, and **process goals** refer to the sequence of events instrumental in achieving outcome goals. **Group processing** may be defined as reflecting on a group session to (a) describe what member actions were helpful and unhelpful and (b) make decisions about what actions to continue or change. The purpose of group processing is to clarify and improve the effectiveness of the members in contributing to the collaborative efforts to achieve the group's goals. Groups need to describe what member actions were helpful and unhelpful in completing the group's work and make decisions about what behaviors to continue or change. Such processing (1) enables learning groups to focus on maintaining good working relationships among members, (2) facilitates the learning of cooperative skills, (3) ensures that members receive feedback on their participation, (4) ensures that students think on the meta-cognitive as well as the cognitive level, and (5) provides the means to celebrate the success of the group

# Table 1.1
# What Is the Difference?

| Cooperative Learning Groups | Traditional Learning Groups |
| --- | --- |
| Positive interdependence | No interdependence |
| Individual accountability | No individual accountability |
| Heterogenous membership | Homogeneous membership |
| Shared leadership | One appointed leader |
| Responsible for each other | Responsible only for self |
| Task & maintenace emphasized | Only task emphasized |
| Social skills directly taught | Social skills assumed & ignored |
| Teacher observes & intervenes | Teacher ignores groups |
| Group processing occurs | No group processing |

and reinforce the positive behaviors of group members. Some of the keys to successful processing are allowing sufficient time for it to take place, emphasizing positive feedback, making the processing specific rather than vague, maintaining student involvement in processing, reminding students to use their cooperative skills while they process, and communicating clear expectations as to the purpose of processing.

Besides having each learning group process, teachers may lead whole-class processing. When cooperative learning groups are used, the teacher observes the groups, analyzes the problems they have working together, and gives feedback to each group on how well they are working together. An important aspect of both small-group and whole-class processing is group and class celebrations. It is feeling successful, appreciated, and respected that builds commitment to learning and a sense of self- efficacy.

# Back to the Basics

The importance of cooperative learning goes beyond maximizing outcomes such as achievement, positive attitudes toward subject areas, and the ability to think critically, although these are worthwhile outcomes. Knowledge and skills are of no use if the student cannot apply them in cooperative interaction with other people. Being able to perform technical skills such as reading, speaking, listening, writing, computing, and problem-solving are valuable but of little use if the person cannot apply those skills in cooperative interaction with other people. It does no good to train an engineer, secretary, accountant, teacher, or mechanic if the person does not have the cooperative skills needed to apply the knowledge and technical skills in cooperative relationships on the job.

Much of what students learn in school is worthless in the real world. Schools teach that work means performing tasks largely by oneself, helping and assisting others is cheating, technical competencies are the other thing that matters, attendance and punctuality are secondary to test scores, motivation is up to the teacher, success depends on performance on individual tests, and promotions are received no matter how little one works. In the real world of work, things are altogether different. Most employers do not expect people to sit in rows and compete with colleagues without interacting with them. The heart of most jobs, especially the higher-paying more interesting jobs, is teamwork, which involves getting others to cooperate, leading others, coping with complex power and influence issues, and helping solve people's problems in working with each other. Teamwork, communication, effective coordination, and divisions of labor characterize most real-life settings. It is time for schools to leave the ivory tower of working alone and sitting in rows to see who is best and more realistically reflect the realities of adult life.

Students increasingly live in a world characterized by interdependence, pluralism, conflict, and rapid change. Because of technological, economic, ecological, and political interdependence, the solution of most problems cannot be achieved by one country alone. The major problems faced by individuals (e.g., contamination of the environment, warming of the atmosphere, world hunger, international terrorism, nuclear war) are increasing ones that cannot be solved by actions taken only at the national level. Our students will live in a complex, interconnected world in which cultures collide every minute and dependencies limit the flexibility of individuals and nations. The internationalization of problems will increase so that there will be no clear division between domestic and international problems. Students need to learn the competencies involved in managing interdependence, resolving conflicts within cooperative systems made up of parties from different countries and cultures, and personally adapting to rapid change.

Quality of life depends on having close friends who last a lifetime, building and maintaining a loving family, being a responsible parent, caring about others, and contributing to the well-being of the world. These are things that make life worthwhile. Grades in school do not predict which students will have a high quality of life after they are graduated. The ability to work cooperatively with others does. The ability of students to work collaboratively with others is the keystone to building and maintaining the caring and committed relationships that largely determine quality of life.

Despite the importance of cooperative learning experiences, there are critics who challenge its use. They wish to know if the claims of advocates are really valid. In the next chapter, therefore, we shall review briefly the voluminous body of research that has validated the instructional use of cooperation.

# Final Note

During one very difficult trek across an ice field in Don Bennett's hop to the top of Mount Rainer, his daughter stayed by his side for four hours and with each new hop told him, "You can do it, Dad. You're the best dad in the world. You can do it, Dad." There was no way Bennett would quit hopping to the top with his daughter yelling words of love and encouragement in his ear. The encouragement of his daughter kept him going, strengthening his commitment to make it to the top. The classroom is similar. With members of their cooperative group cheering them on, students amaze themselves and their teachers with what they can achieve.

# Chapter 2

# Research On Cooperative Learning

Linda Scott, in her Moundsview, Minnesota 5th-grade classroom, assigns her students a set of math story problems to solve. She assigns her students to groups of three, ensuring that a high-, medium-, and low-performing math students and both male and female students in each group. The instructional task is to solve each story problem correctly and to understand the correct process for doing so. Each group is given a set of story problems (one copy for each student) and a set of three "role" cards. Each group member is assigned one of the roles. The **reader** reads the problem aloud to the group. The **checker** makes sure that all members can explain how to solve each problem correctly. The **encourager** in a friendly way encourages all members of the group to participate in the discussion, sharing their ideas and feelings.

Within this lesson **positive interdependence** is structured by the group agreeing on (1) the answer and (2) the process for solving each problem. Since the group certifies that each member (1) has the correct answer written on their answer sheet and (2) can correctly explain how to solve each problem, **individual account-ability** is structured by having the teacher pick one answer sheet at random to score for the group and to ask randomly one group member to explain how to solve one of the problems. The **cooperative skills** emphasized in the lesson are checking and encouraging. Finally, at the end of the period the groups **process** their functioning by answering two questions: (1) What is something each member did that was helpful for the group and (2) What is something each member could do to make the group even better tomorrow?

As a result of structuring this math lesson cooperatively, what instructional outcomes can the teacher expect?

Working together to get the job done can have profound effects on students and staff members. A great deal of research has been conducted on the relationship among cooperative, competitive, and individualistic efforts and instructional outcomes (Johnson & Johnson, 1974, 1978, 1983, 1989a; Johnson, Nelson, & Maruyama, 1983; Johnson, Maruyama, Johnson, Nelson, & Skon, 1981; Pepitone, 1980; Sharan, 1980; Slavin, 1983). These research studies began in the late 1890's when Triplett (1897) in the United States, Turner (1889) in England, and Mayer (1903) in Germany conducted a series of studies on the factors associated with competitive performance. The amount of research that has been conducted since is staggering. During the past 90 years over 600 studies have been conducted by a wide variety of researchers in different decades with different age subjects, in different subject areas, and in different settings. We know far more about the efficacy of cooperative learning than we know about lecturing, age grouping, beginning reading instruction at age six, departmentalization, or almost any other facet of education. While there is not space enough in this chapter to review all of the research, a comprehensive review of all studies may be found in Johnson and Johnson (1989a). In most cases, references to individual studies are not included in this chapter. Rather, the reader is referred to reviews that contain the references to the specific studies that corroborate the point being made.

Building on the theorizing of Kurt Lewin and Morton Deutsch, the premise may be made that the type of interdependence structured among students determines how they interact with each other which, in turn largely determines instructional outcomes. The quality of peer relationships, furthermore, has widespread and powerful impact on individuals' cognitive and social development. In this chapter, therefore, the importance of high quality peer relationships, student-student interaction patterns, and the instructional outcomes promoted by the three goal structures are discussed.

# Importance of Peer Relationships

Children and adolescents live in an expanding social world. From relating primarily to adult caretakers, young children begin interacting with other adults and with other children. As children become older, they have more interaction with other children and less interaction with adults. Yet, traditionally, adults in the United States have viewed the interaction between adults and children as the most important vehicle for ensuring the effective socialization and development of children and adolescents. Child-child relationships have been assumed to be, at best, relatively unimportant and, at worst, unhealthy influences.

This adult-centric view is reflected in the policies of our schools. In schools most legitimate peer interaction among students has been limited to extracurricular activities. These activities rarely deal directly with the basic issues of classroom life. The system of instruction emphasizes teacher lectures and seatwork done by students individualistically. Student attempts to interact with each other are seen as disruptive of this system. Furthermore, the rigid age segregation usually applied in school classrooms (and also fostered by the subdividing of school programs for administrative purposes into elementary, junior, and senior high schools) often limits peer interaction within a narrowly confined age span. Finally, educators systematically fail to train students in the basic social skills necessary for interacting effectively with peers (in this chapter the word **peer** means a wide range of other children or adolescents). These skills are not considered pedagogically useful. Essentially, the typical adult-child dyadic view of teaching and learning has deemphasized student- student relationships in the classroom.

Despite these patterns of deemphasis, **peer relationships are a critical element in the development and socialization of children and adolescents** (Hartup, 1976; Johnson, 1980). In fact, the primary relationships in which development and socialization may take place may be with peers. Compared with interactions with adults, interactions with peers tend to be more frequent, intense, and varied throughout childhood and adolescence. Experiences with peers are not superficial luxuries to be enjoyed during lunch or on a Saturday afternoon. Constructive relationships with peers are a necessity.

There are numerous ways in which peer relationships contribute to (1) social and cognitive development and (2) socialization. Some of the more important consequences correlated with peer relationships are (the specific supporting evidence may be found in Johnson, 1980, and Johnson & Johnson, in press):

1. **In their interactions with peers, children and adolescents directly learn attitudes, values, skills, and information unobtainable from adults.** In their interactions with each other, children and adolescents imitate each other's behavior and identify with friends possessing admired competencies. Through providing models, reinforcement, and direct learning, peers shape a wide variety of social behaviors, attitudes, and perspectives.

2. **Interaction with peers provides support, opportunities, and models for prosocial behavior.** It is within interactions with other children and adolescents that one helps, comforts, shares with, takes care of, assists, and gives to others. Without peers with whom to engage in such behaviors, many forms of prosocial values and commitments could not be developed. Conversely, whether adolescents engage in problem or transition behavior, such as the use of illegal drugs and delinquency, is related to the perceptions of their friends' attitudes toward such behaviors. Being rejected by one's peers tends to result in antisocial behavioral patterns characterized by aggressiveness, disruptiveness, and other negatively perceived behavior.

3. Children and adolescents frequently lack the time perspective needed to tolerate delays in gratification. As they develop and are socialized, the focus on their own immediate impulses and needs is replaced with the ability to take longer perspectives. **Peers provide models of, expectations of, directions for, and reinforcements of learning to control impulses.** Aggressive impulses provide an example. Peer interaction involving such activities as rough-and-tumble play

promotes the acquisition of a repertoire of effective aggressive behaviors and helps establish the necessary regulatory mechanisms for modulating aggressive effect.

4. **Children and adolescents learn to view situations and problems from perspectives other than their own through their interaction with peers.** Such perspective taking is one of the most critical competencies for cognitive and social development. All psychological development may be described as a progressive loss of egocentrism and an increase in ability to take wider and more complex perspectives. It is primarily in interaction with peers that egocentrism is lost and increased perspective taking is gained.

5. **Autonomy** is the ability to understand what others expect in any given situation and to be free to choose whether to meet their expectations. Autonomous people are independent of both extreme inner- or outer-directedness. When making decisions concerning appropriate social behavior, autonomous people tend to consider both their internal values and the situational requirements and then respond in flexible and appropriate ways. Autonomy is the result of (1) the internalization of values (including appropriate self- approval) derived from caring and supportive relationships, and (2) the acquisition of social skills and sensitivity. **Relationships with other children and adolescents are powerful influences on the development of the values and the social sensitivity required for autonomy.** Children with a history of isolation from or rejection by peers, furthermore, often are inappropriately other directed. They conform to group pressures even when they believe the recommended actions are wrong or inappropriate.

6. While adults can provide certain forms of companionship, **children need close and intimate relationships with peers with whom they can share their thoughts and feelings, aspirations and hopes, dreams and fantasies, and joys and pains.** Children need constructive peer relationships to avoid the pain of loneliness.

7. Throughout infancy, childhood, adolescence, and early adulthood, a person moves through several successive and overlapping identities. The physical changes involved in growth, the increasing number of experiences with other people, increasing responsibilities, and general cognitive and social development all cause changes in self-definition. The final result should be a coherent and integrated identity. In peer relationships children and adolescents become aware of the similarities and differences between themselves and others. They experiment with a variety of social roles that help them integrate their own sense of self. In peer relationships values and attitudes are clarified and integrated into an individual's self-definition. **It is through peer relationships that a frame of reference for perceiving oneself is developed.** Gender typing and its impact on one's identity is an example.

8. **Coalitions formed during childhood and adolescence provide help and assistance throughout adulthood.**

9. The ability to maintain interdependent, cooperative relationships is a prime manifestation of psychological health. Poor peer relationships in elementary school predict psychological disturbance and delinquency in high school, and poor peer relationships in high school predict adult pathology. **The absence of any friendships during childhood and adolescence seems to increase the risk of mental disorder.**

10. **In both educational and work settings, peers have a strong influence on productivity.** Greater achievement is typically found in collaborative situations where peers work together than in situations where individuals work alone. Especially when a child or adolescent has poor study skills or is unmotivated, cooperative interaction with peers has powerful effects on productivity. Supportive relationships with peers are also related to using one's abilities in achievement situations.

11. **Student educational aspirations may be more influenced by peers than by any other social influence.** Similarly, ambition in career settings is greatly influenced by peers.

Within instructional situations, peer relationships can be structured to create meaningful interdependence through learning cooperatively with peers. Within cooperative learning situations students experience feelings of belonging, acceptance, support, and caring, and the social skills and social roles required for maintaining interdependent relationships can be taught and practiced.

Through repeated cooperative experiences students can develop the social sensitivity of what behavior is expected from others and the actual skills and autonomy to meet such expectations if they so desire. Through holding each other accountable for appropriate social behavior, students can greatly influence the values they internalize and the self-control they develop. It is through belonging to a series of interdependent relationships that values are learned and internalized. It is through prolonged cooperative interaction with other people that healthy social development with the overall balance of trust rather than distrust of other people, the ability to view situations and problems from a variety of perspectives, a meaningful sense of direction and purpose in life, an awareness of mutual interdependence with others, and an integrated and coherent sense of personal identity, takes place (Johnson, 1979; Johnson & Matross, 1977).

**In order for peer relationships to be constructive influences, they must promote feelings of belonging, acceptance, support, and caring, rather than feelings of hostility and rejection** (Johnson. 1980). Being accepted by peers is related to willingness to engage in social interaction, utilizing abilities in achievement situations, and providing positive social rewards for peers. Isolation from peers is associated with high anxiety, low self- esteem, poor interpersonal skills, emotional handicaps, and psychological pathology. Rejection by peers is related to disruptive classroom behavior, hostile behavior and negative affect, and negative attitudes toward other students and school. In order to promote constructive peer influences, therefore, teachers must first ensure that students interact with each other and, second, must ensure that the interaction takes place within a cooperative context.

## Summary

Educators who wish to promote constructive relationships among students will wish to (Johnson & Johnson, 1980):

1. Structure cooperative situations in which children and adolescents work with peers to achieve a common goal.

2. Emphasize joint rather than individual products whenever possible.

3. Directly teach the interpersonal skills needed to build and maintain collaborative relationships with peers.

4. Give children and adolescents meaningful responsibility for the well-being and success of their peers.

5. Encourage the feelings of support, acceptance, concern, and commitment that are part of collaborative situations.

6. Hold children and adolescents accountable for fulfilling their obligations and responsibilities to their collaborators and give them mutual authority over each other.

7. Ensure that students experience success in working cooperatively with peers.

# Interaction Patterns

Simply placing students near each other and allowing interaction to take place does not mean that high quality peer relationships will result and that learning will be maximized. The nature of interaction is important. Some interaction leads to students rejecting each other and defensively avoiding being influenced by peers. When student-student interaction leads to relationships characterized by perceived support and acceptance, then the potential effects described in the previous section are likely to be found.

There have been several hundred studies comparing the effects of cooperative, competitive, and individualistic goal structures on aspects of interpersonal interaction important for learning (see Johnson & Johnson, 1989a). A cooperative goal structure leads to a promotive interaction pattern among students. **Promotive interaction** occurs as individuals encouraging and facilitating each other's efforts to achieve. It is characterized by personal and academic acceptance and support, exchange of information, mutual help and assistance, high intrinsic achievement motivation, and high emotional involvement in learning.

A competitive goal structure results in an oppositional pattern of student-student interaction. **Oppositional interaction** occurs as individuals discouraging and obstructing each other's efforts to achieve. It results in rejection of classmates, obstruction of each other's work, avoidance of information exchange or communication, low achievement motivation, and psychological withdrawal and avoidance. The negative interdependence created by a competitive goal structure results in students having a vested interest in obstructing one another's learning. There are two ways to win in a competition--to do better than anyone else or to prevent anyone else from doing better than you. This is known as a good offense and a good defense. In a classroom, however, preventing against classmates learning more than you can create destructive interaction patterns that decrease learning for everyone.

An individualistic goal structure results in no interaction among students. **No interdependence** exists when individuals work independently without any interchange with each other. Students work alone without bothering their classmates. Such a goal structure minimizes peer relationships and interaction in learning situations.

## Acceptance, Support, Trust, Liking

If you want students to encourage and support each other's efforts to achieve, and if you wish students to accept and trust each other, cooperative learning should dominate your classroom. Cooperative learning experiences, compared with competitive and individualistic ones, have been found to result in stronger beliefs that other students (and teachers) care about how much one learns and want to help one learn (Johnson & Johnson, 1989a). Furthermore, cooperative attitudes are related to mutual acceptance, respect, liking, and trust among students.

From Table 2.1 it may be seen that cooperation resulted in greater social support than did competitive or individualistic efforts (effect sizes of 0.59 and 0.71 respectively). Social support tends to be related to (see Johnson & Johnson, 1989a):

1. Achievement, successful problem solving, persistence on challenging tasks under frustrating conditions, lack of cognitive interference during problem solving, lack of absenteeism, academic and career aspirations, more appropriate seeking of assistance, retention, job satisfaction, high morale, and greater compliance with regimens and behavioral patterns that increase health and productivity.

2. Living a longer life, recovering from illness and injury faster and more completely, and experiencing less severe illnesses.

3. Psychological health and adjustment, lack of neuroticism and psychopathology, reduction of psychological distress, coping effectively with stressful situations, self- reliance and autonomy, a coherent and integrated self-identity, greater psychological safety, higher self-esteem, increased general happiness, and increased interpersonal skills.

4. Effective management of stress by providing the caring, information, resources, and feedback individuals need to cope with stress, by reducing the number and severity of stressful events in an individual's life, by reducing anxiety, and by helping one appraise the nature of the stress and one's ability to deal with it constructively.

5. The emotional support and encouragement individuals need to cope with the risk that is inherently involved in

challenging one's competence and striving to grow and develop.

The importance of social support has been ignored within education over the past 30 years. **A general principle to keep in mind is that the pressure to achieve should always be matched with an equal level of social support.** Challenge and support must be kept in balance. Whenever increased demands and pressure to be productive are placed on students (and teachers), a corresponding increase in social support should be structured.

## Exchange of Information

The seeking of information, and utilizing it in one's learning, is essential for academic achievement. Students working within a cooperative goal structure (Johnson & Johnson, 1989a):

1. Seek significantly more information from each other than do students working within a competitive goal structure.

2. Are less biased and have fewer misperceptions in comprehending the viewpoints and positions of other individuals.

3. More accurately communicate information by verbalizing ideas and information more frequently , attending to others' statements more carefully, and accepting others' ideas and information more frequently.

4. Are more confident about the value of their ideas.

5. Make optimal use of the information provided by other students.

## Motivation

**Motivation is most commonly viewed as a combination of the perceived likelihood of success and the perceived incentive for success.** The greater the likelihood of success and the more important it is to succeed, the higher the motivation. Success that is intrinsically rewarding is usually seen as being more desirable for learning than is having students believe that only extrinsic rewards are worthwhile. There is greater perceived likelihood of success and success is viewed as more important in cooperative than in competitive or individualistic learning situations (Johnson & Johnson, 1989a). In addition, cooperative learning tends to generate intrinsic motivation to learn while competitive and individualistic learning tend to be fueled by extrinsic motivation. Finally, students tend to be more emotionally involved in cooperative than in competitive or individualistic learning activities.

# Learning Outcomes

Different learning outcomes result from the student-student interaction patterns promoted by the use of cooperative, competitive, and individualistic goal structures (Johnson & Johnson 1989a). While space is too short here to review all of the research, some of the major findings are as follows.

## Cooperative Efforts And Achievement / Productivity

> *"The highest and best form of efficiency is the spontaneous cooperation of a free people."*

> Woodrow Wilson

How successful competitive, individualistic, and cooperative efforts are in promoting productivity and achievement is the first question pragmatists ask about social interdependence. Over 375 studies have been conducted over the past 90 years to give an answer (Johnson & Johnson, 1989a). When all of the studies were included in the analysis, the average cooperator performed at about 2/3 a standard deviation above average student learning within a competitive (effect size = 0.66) or individualistic situation (effect size = 0.63). When only the high-quality studies were included in the analysis, the effect sizes are 0.86 and 0.59 respectively. Cooperative learning, furthermore, resulted in more higher-level reasoning, more frequent generation of new ideas and solutions (i.e., **process gain**), and greater transfer of what is learned within one situation to another (i.e., **group-to- individual transfer**) than did competitive or individualistic learning.

Some cooperative learning procedures contained a mixture of cooperative, competitive, and individualistic efforts while others are "pure." The original jigsaw procedure (Aronson, et al., 1978), for example, is a combination of resource interdependence (cooperative) and individual reward structures (individualistic). Teams-Games- Tournaments (DeVries & Edwards, 1974) and Student-Teams- Achievement-Divisions (Slavin, 1980) are mixtures of cooperation and intergroup competition. Team- Assisted-Instruction (Slavin, Leavey, & Madden, 1983) is a mixture of individualistic and cooperative learning. When the results of "pure" and "mixed" operationalizations of cooperative learning were compared, the "pure" operationalizations produced higher achievement.

Since research participants have varied widely as to economic class, age, sex, and cultural background, since a wide variety of research tasks and measures of the dependent variables have been used, and since the research has been conducted by many different researchers with markedly different orientations working in different settings and in different decades, the overall body of research on social interdependence has considerable generalizability.

That working together to achieve a common goal produces higher achievement and greater productivity than does working alone is so well confirmed by so much research that it stands as one of the strongest principles of social and organizational psychology. Cooperative learning is indicated whenever the learning goals are highly important, mastery and retention is important, the task is complex or conceptual, problem solving is desired, divergent thinking or creativity is desired, quality of performance is expected, and higher level reasoning strategies and critical thinking are needed.

# Table 2:1
# Social Interdependence: Weighted Findings

|  | Mean | s.d. | n |
|---|---|---|---|
| **Achievement** | | | |
| Cooperative vs. Competitive | 0.66 | 0.94 | 128 |
| Cooperative vs. Individualistic | 0.63 | 0.81 | 182 |
| Competitive vs. Individualistic | 0.30 | 0.76 | 39 |
| **Interpersonal Attraction** | | | |
| Cooperative vs. Competitive | 0.65 | 0.47 | 88 |
| Cooperative vs. Individualistic | 0.62 | 0.59 | 59 |
| Competitive vs. Individualistic | 0.08 | 0.70 | 15 |
| **Social Support** | | | |
| Cooperative vs. Competitive | 0.59 | 0.39 | 75 |
| Cooperative vs. Individualistic | 0.71 | 0.45 | 70 |
| Competitive vs. Individualistic | -0.12 | 0.37 | 18 |
| **Self-Esteem** | | | |
| Cooperative vs. Competitive | 0.60 | 0.56 | 55 |
| Cooperative vs. Individualistic | 0.44 | 0.40 | 37 |
| Competitive vs. Individualistic | -0.19 | 0.40 | 18 |

## What Mediates?

Why does cooperation result in higher achievement--what
mediates? The critical issue in understanding the relationship between cooperation and achievement is specifying the variables
that mediate the relationship. Simply placing students in groups
and telling them to work together does not in and of itself
promote higher achievement. It is only under certain conditions
that group efforts may be expected to be more productive than
individual efforts. Those conditions are:

1. **Clearly perceived positive interdependence.** From the research, it may be concluded that positive interdependence
   provides the context within which promotive interaction takes
   place, group membership and interpersonal interaction

among students do not produce higher achievement unless positive interdependence is clearly structured, the combination of goal and reward interdependence increases achievement over goal interdependence alone, and resource interdependence does not increase achievement unless goal interdependence is present also (Johnson & Johnson, 1989a).

2. **Considerable promotive (face-to-face) interaction.** Within cooperative learning, compared with competitive and individualistic learning, students (a) provide others with efficient and effective help and assistance, (b) exchange needed resources such as information and materials and processing information more efficiently and effectively, (c) provide each other with feedback in order to improve their subsequent performance on assigned tasks and responsibilities, (d) challenge each other's conclusions and reasoning in order to promote higher quality decision making and greater insight into the problems being considered, (e) advocate exerting efforts to achieve mutual goals, (f) influence each other's efforts to achieve mutual goals, (g) act in trusting and trustworthy ways, (h) are motivated to strive for mutual benefit, and (i) feel less anxiety and stress (Johnson & Johnson, 1989a).

3. **Felt personal responsibility (individual accountability) to achieve the group's goals.** When groups work on tasks where it is difficult to identify members' contributions, when there is an increased likelihood of redundant efforts, and when there is lessened responsibility for the final outcome, the less some members will try to contribute to goal achievement. If, however, there is high individual accountability and it is clear how much effort each member is contributing, if redundant efforts are avoided, if every member is responsible for the final outcome, then the social loafing effect vanishes (Johnson & Johnson, 1989a). The smaller the size of the group the greater the individual accountability may be.

4. **Frequent use of relevant interpersonal and small group skills.** Social skills and competencies tend to increase more within cooperative than in competitive or individualistic situations (Johnson & Johnson, 1989a). Working together to get

the job done requires students to provide leadership, build and maintain trust, communicate effectively, and manage conflicts constructively. The more socially skillful students are, and the more attention teachers pay to teaching and rewarding the use of social skills, the higher the achievement that can be expected within cooperative learning groups. In their studies on the long-term implementation of cooperative learning, Lew and Mesch (Lew, Mesch, Johnson, & Johnson, 1986a, 1986b; Mesch, Johnson, & Johnson, 1988; Mesch, Lew, Johnson, & Johnson, 1986) investigated the impact of a reward contingency for using social skills as well as positive interdependence and a contingency for academic achievement on performance within cooperative learning groups. In the cooperative skills conditions students were trained weekly in four social skills and each member of a cooperative group was given two bonus points toward the quiz grade if all group members were observed by the teacher to demonstrate three out of four cooperative skills. The results indicated that the combination of positive interdependence, an academic contingency for high performance by all group members, and a social skills contingency, promoted the highest achievement.

5. **Periodic and regular group processing.** Stuart Yager examined the impact on achievement of (a) cooperative learning in which members discussed how well their group was functioning and how they could improve its effectiveness, (b) cooperative learning without any group processing, and (c) individualistic learning (Yager, Johnson, & Johnson, 1985). The results indicate that the high-, medium-, and low-achieving students in the cooperation with group processing condition achieved higher on daily achievement, post-instructional achievement, and retention measures than did the students in the other two conditions. Students in the cooperation without group processing condition, furthermore, achieved higher on all three measures than did the students in the individualistic condition. Johnson, Johnson, Stanne, and Garibaldi (in press) conducted a follow-up study comparing cooperative learning with no processing, cooperative learning with teacher processing (teacher specified cooperative skills to use, observed, and gave whole class feedback as to how well stu-

dents were using the skills), cooperative learning with teacher and student processing (teacher specified cooperative skills to use, observed, gave whole class feedback as to how well students were using the skills, and had learning groups discuss how well they interacted as a group), and individualistic learning. Forty-nine high ability Black American high school seniors and entering college freshmen at Xavier University participated in the study. A complex computer- assisted problem-solving assignment was given to all students. All three cooperative conditions performed higher than did the individualistic condition. The combination of teacher and student processing resulted in greater problem-solving success than did the other cooperative conditions.

## Critical Thinking Competencies

In many subject areas related to science and technology the teaching of facts and theories is considered to be secondary to the teaching of critical thinking and the use of higher level reasoning strategies. The aim of science education, for example, has been to develop individuals "who can sort sense from nonsense," or who have the critical thinking abilities of grasping information, examining it, evaluating it for soundness, and applying it appropriately. Cooperative learning promotes a greater use of higher reasoning strategies and critical thinking than do competitive and individualistic learning strategies (Johnson & Johnson, 1989a).

United States' students frequently believe that a learning task is completed when they have an answer in every blank in a worksheet. Sustained effort to comprehend material deeply seems to be rare. The Japanese, on the other hand, view academic success as a matter of disciplined, enduring effort aimed at achieving **satori**, or the sudden flash of enlightenment that comes after long, intensive, but successful effort. The achievement of satori is much more likely after a discussion in cooperative learning groups than after working alone, competitively, or individualistically to complete an assignment.

## Attitudes Toward Subject Area

Cooperative learning experiences, compared with competitive and individualistic ones, promote more positive attitudes toward the subject area, more positive attitudes toward the instructional experience, and more continuing motivation to learn more about the subject area being studied (Johnson & Johnson, 1989a). These findings have important implications, for example, for influencing female and minority students to enter science and math oriented careers.

# Interpersonal Relationships

Cooperative learning experiences, compared with competitive, individualistic, and "traditional instruction," promote considerably more liking among students (effect sizes = 0.65 and 0.62 respectively) (Johnson & Johnson, 1989a; Johnson, Johnson, & Maruyama, 1983). This is true regardless of differences in ability level, sex, handicapping conditions, ethnic membership, social class differences, or task orientation. Students who collaborate on their studies develop considerable commitment and caring for each other no matter what their initial impressions of and attitudes toward each other were. They also like the teacher better and perceive the teacher as being more supportive and accepting academically and personally.

In order to be productive, a class of students (or a school faculty) has to cohere and have a positive emotional climate. As relationships become more positive, absenteeism decreases, and increases may be expected in student commitment to learning, feelings of personal responsibility to do the assigned work, willingness to take on difficult tasks, motivation and persistence in working on learning tasks, satisfaction and morale, willingness to endure pain and frustration to succeed, willingness to defend the school against external criticism or attack, willingness to listen to and be influenced by peers, commitment to peer's success and growth, and productivity and achievement (Johnson & F. Johnson, 1987; Watson & Johnson, 1972). In addition, when students are heterogeneous with regard to ethnic, social class, language, and ability differences, cooperative learning experiences are a necessity for building positive peer relationships.

# Psychological Health

When students leave school, we would hope that they would have the psychological health and stability required to build and maintain career, family, and community relationships, to establish a basic and meaningful interdependence with other people, and to participate effectively in our society. Our studies (Johnson & Johnson, 1989a) indicate that **cooperativeness** is positively related to a number of indices of psychological health, namely: emotional maturity, well-adjusted social relations, strong personal identity, and basic trust in and optimism about people. **Competitiveness** seems also to be related to a number of indices of psychological health, while **individualistic attitudes** tend to be related to a number of indices of psychological pathology, emotional immaturity, social maladjustment, delinquency, self-alienation, and self-rejection. To the degree that schools can contribute to a student's psychological well-being, they should be organized to reinforce those traits and tendencies that promote it.

## Accuracy of Perspective Taking

**Social perspective taking** is the ability to understand how a situation appears to another person and how that person is reacting cognitively and emotionally to the situation. The opposite of perspective taking is **egocentrism**, the embeddedness in one's own viewpoint to the extent that one is unaware of other points of view and of the limitations of one's perspectives. Cooperative learning experiences tend to promote greater cognitive and affective perspective taking than do competitive or individualistic learning experiences (Johnson & Johnson, 1989a).

## Self-Esteem

The data in Table 2.1 indicate that cooperation produced higher levels of self-esteem than did competitive and individualistic efforts (effect-sizes of 0.60 and 0.44 respectively). Individuals with low self-esteem tend to (Johnson & Johnson, 1989a):

1. Have low productivity due to setting low goals for themselves, lacking confidence in their ability, and assuming that they will fail no matter how hard they try.

2. Be critical of others as well as themselves by looking for flaws in others and trying to "tear them down."

3. Withdraw socially due to feeling awkward, self-conscious, and vulnerable to rejection.

4. Be conforming, agreeable, highly persuasible, and highly influenced by criticism.

5. Develop more psychological problems such as anxiety, nervousness, insomnia, depression, and psychosomatic symptoms.

Within **competitive** situations self-esteem tends to be based on the contingent view of one's competence that, "If I win, then I have worth as a person, but if I lose, then I have no worth." Winners attribute their success to superior ability and attribute the failure of others to lack of ability, both of which contribute to self-aggrandizement. Losers, who are the vast majority, defensively tend to be self-disparaging, apprehensive about evaluation, and tend to withdraw psychologically and physically. Within **individualistic** situations, students are isolated from one another, receive little direct comparison with or feedback from peers, and perceive evaluations as inaccurate and unrealistic. A defensive avoidance, evaluation apprehension, and distrust of peers results. Within **cooperative** situations, individuals tend to interact, promote each other's success, form multi-dimensional and realistic impressions of each other's competencies, and give accurate feedback. Such interaction tends to promote a basic self-acceptance of oneself as a competent person.

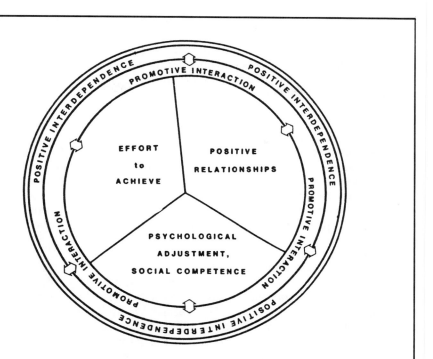

**Figure 2.1 Outcomes Of Cooperation**

# Relationships Among Outcomes

**There are bidirectional relationships among achievement, quality of interpersonal relationships, and psychological health** (Johnson & Johnson, 1989a). Each influences the others. Caring and committed friendships come from a sense of mutual accomplishment, mutual pride in joint work, and the bonding that results from joint efforts. The more students care about each other, on the other hand, the harder they will work to achieve mutual learning goals. Long-term and persistent efforts to achieve do not come from the head, they come from the heart (Johnson & Johnson, 1989b). Individuals seek out opportunities to work with those they care about. As caring increases, so do feelings of personal responsibility to do one's share of the work, willingness to take on difficult tasks, motivation and persistence in working toward goal achievement, and willingness to endure pain and frustration on behalf of the group. All these contribute to group productivity.

In addition, the joint success experienced in working together to get the job done enhances social competencies, self-esteem, and general psychological health. The healthier psychologically individuals are, on the other hand, the better able they are to work with others to achieve mutual goals. Joint efforts require coordination, effective communication, leadership, and conflict management. States of depression, anxiety, guilt, shame, and anger decrease the energy available to contribute to a cooperative effort.

Finally, the more positive interpersonal relationships are, the greater the psychological health of the individuals involved. Through the internalization of positive relationships, direct social support, shared intimacy, and expressions of caring, psychological health and the ability to cope with stress are built. The absence of caring and committed relationships and destructive relationships tend to increase psychological pathology. On the other hand, states of depression, anxiety, guilt, shame, and anger decrease individuals' ability to build and maintain caring and committed relationships. The healthier psychologically individuals are, the more meaningful and caring the relationships they can build and maintain.

# Reducing The Discrepancy

With the amount of research evidence available, it is surprising that classroom practice is so oriented toward individualistic and competitive learning and schools are so dominated by a competitive / individualistic structure. **It is time for the discrepancy to be reduced between what research indicates is effective in teaching and what teachers actually do.** In order to do so, educators must understand the role of the teacher in implementing cooperative learning experiences. That is the focus of the next chapter.

# Chapter 3

# The Teacher's Role In Cooperative Learning

## Introduction

At this point you know what cooperative learning is and how it is different from competitive and individualistic learning. You know that the research supports the propositions that cooperation results in greater effort to achieve, more positive interpersonal relationships, and greater psychological health and self-esteem than do competitive or individualistic efforts. You know that **the essence of cooperative learning is positive interdependence** where students recognize that "we are in this together, sink or swim." Other essential components include individual accountability (where every student is accountable for both learning the assigned material and helping other group members learn), face-to-face interaction among students within which students promote each other's success, students appropriately using interpersonal and group skills, and students processing how effectively their learning group has functioned. These five essential components of cooperation form the conceptual basis for constructing cooperative procedures. In addition, however, teachers need to understand how to implement the essential components of cooperation within the teacher's role.

## The Teacher's Role

When Roger was teaching fourth grade in Jefferson County, Colorado, one of his favorite science lessons was to ask the class to determine how long a candle burns in a quart jar. He assigned students to groups of two, making the pairs as heterogeneous as he could. Each pair was given one candle and one quart jar. He gave the instructional task of timing how long the candle would burn. Students then lit their candle, placed the quart jar over it, and clocked how long the candle burns. They were expected to share the materials and praise each other's work. The answers from the pairs are then announced. Roger then gave the pairs the task of generating a number of answers to the question, "How many factors make a difference in how long the candle burns in the jar?" The answers from the pairs were written on the board. The pairs were then assigned the task of repeating the experiment in ways that tested which of the suggested factors did in fact make a difference in how long the candle burned. The next day students individually took a quiz on the factors affecting the time a candle would burn in a quart jar and their scores were summed together to determine a joint score. They spent some time discussing the helpful actions of each member and what they could do to be even more effective in the future.

In this lesson **positive interdependence** was structured by requiring one answer from the pair and by the assignment of one set of materials to each group. There was constant **face-to-face interaction** between pair members. **Individual accountability** was structured by the individual quiz given after the experiments were carried out. The **collaborative skills** emphasized included sharing materials and ideas and praising. The pairs **processed** how effectively they functioned.

Science experiments are only one of the many places cooperative learning may be used. Cooperative learning is appropriate for any instructional task. The more conceptual the task, the more problem solving and decision making that are required, and the more creative the answers need to be, the greater the superiority of cooperative over competitive and individualistic learning. Whenever the learning goals are highly important, the task is complex or conceptual, problem solving is desired, divergent thinking or creativity is desired, quality of performance is expected, higher level reasoning strategies and critical thinking are needed, long-term retention is desired, or when the social development of students is one of the major instructional goals-- cooperative learning should be used.

Within cooperative learning situations, the teacher, besides being a technical/subject-matter expert, is a classroom manager and consultant to promote effective group functioning. The teacher structures the learning groups, teaches the basic concepts and strategies, and then monitors the functioning of the learning groups and intervenes to teach collaborative skills and provide task assistance when it is needed. Students are taught to look to their peers for assistance, feedback, reinforcement, and support. Students are expected to interact with each other, share ideas and materials, support and encourage academic achievement, orally explain and elaborate the concepts being learned, and hold each other accountable for learning. A criterion-referenced evaluation system is used.

There is more to the teacher's role in structuring cooperative learning situations, however, than structuring cooperation among students. The teacher's role includes five major sets of strategies:

1. Clearly specifying the objectives for the lesson.

2. Making certain decisions about placing students in learning groups before the lesson is taught.

3. Clearly explaining the task and goal structure to the students.

4. Monitoring the effectiveness of the cooperative learning groups and intervening to provide task assistance (such as answering questions and teaching task skills) or to increase students' interpersonal and group skills.

5. Evaluating the students' achievement and helping students discuss how well they collaborated with each other.

The following eighteen steps elaborate these strategies and detail a procedure for structuring cooperative learning. Specific examples of lessons may be found in Johnson, Johnson, and

Holubec (1987). There are also two films available demonstrating the use of cooperative learning procedures (**Belonging**, **Circles of Learning**).

# Specifying the Instructional Objectives

There are two types of objectives that a teacher needs to specify before the lesson begins. The **academic objective** needs to be specified at the correct level for the students and matched to the right level of instruction according to a conceptual or task analysis. The **collaborative skills objective** details what collaborative skills are going to be emphasized during the lesson. A common error many teachers make is to specify only academic objectives and to ignore the collaborative skills objectives needed to train students to cooperate with each other.

# Deciding on the Size of the Group

Once the objectives of the lesson are clear, the teacher must decide which size of learning group is optimal. Cooperative learning groups tend to range in size from 2 to 6. A number of factors should be considered in selecting the size of a cooperative learning group:

1. **As the size of the learning group increases, the range of abilities, expertise, skills, and the number of minds available for acquiring and processing information increase.** The more group members you have, the more chance to have someone who has special knowledge helpful to the group and the more willing hands and talents are available to do the task.

2. **The larger the group, the more skillful group members must be in providing everyone with a chance to speak, coordinating the actions of group members, reaching consensus, ensuring explanation and elaboration of**

**the material being learned, keeping all members on task, and maintaining good working relationships.** Within a pair students have to manage two interactions. Within a group of three there are six interactions to manage. Within a group of four there are twelve interactions to manage. As the size of the group increases, the interpersonal and small group skills required to manage the interactions among group members become far more complex and sophisticated. Very few students have the social skills needed for effective group functioning even for small groups. A common mistake made by many teachers is to have students work in groups of four, five, and six members before the students have the skills to do so competently.

3. **The materials available or the specific nature of the task may dictate a group size.**

4. **The shorter the period of time available, the smaller the learning group should be.** If there is only a brief period of time available for the lesson, then smaller groups will be more effective because they take less time to get organized, they operate faster, and there is more "air time" per member.

**Our best advice to beginning teachers is to start with pairs or threesomes.** When students become more experienced and skillful they will be able to manage larger groups. Six may be the upper limit for a cooperative learning group. More members would be cumbersome even for very socially skilled students. In one classroom we recently observed the teacher had divided the class into "committees" of eight. In the typical committee some students were being left out, others were passive, and some were engaged in a conversation with only one or two other members. Cooperative learning groups have to be small enough that everyone is engaged in mutual discussion while achieving the group's goals. So be cautious about group size. Some students will not be ready for a group as large as four.

# Assigning Students to Groups

Teachers often ask four basic questions about assigning students to groups:

1. **Should students be placed in learning groups homogeneous or heterogeneous in member ability?** There are times when cooperative learning groups homogeneous in ability may be used to master specific skills or to achieve certain instructional objectives. Generally, however, we recommend that teachers maximize the heterogeneity of students, placing high-, medium-, and low-ability students within the same learning group. More elaborative thinking, more frequent giving and receiving of explanations, and greater perspective taking in discussing material seems to occur in heterogeneous groups, all of which increase the depth of understanding, the quality of reasoning, and the accuracy of long-term retention.

2. **Should nontask-oriented students be placed in learning groups with task-oriented peers or be separated?** To keep nonacademically-oriented students on task it often helps to place them in a cooperative learning group with task-oriented peers.

3. **Should students select whom they want to work with or should the teacher assign students to groups?** Teacher-made groups often have the best mix since teachers can put together optimal combinations of students. Random assignment, such as having students "count off" is another possibility for getting a good mix of students in each group. Having students select their own groups is often not very successful. Student-selected groups often are homogeneous with high-achieving students working with other high-achieving students, white students working with other white students, minority students working with other minority students, and males working with other males. Often there is less on-task behavior in student-selected

than in teacher-selected groups. A useful modification of the "select your own group" method is to have students list whom they would like to work with and then place them in a learning group with one person they choose and one or two or more students that the teacher selected.

4. **How long should the groups stay together?** Actually, there is no formula or simple answer to this question. Some teachers keep cooperative learning groups together for an entire year or semester. Other teachers like to keep a learning group together only long enough to complete a unit or chapter. In some schools student attendance is so unpredictable that teachers form new groups every day. Sooner or later, however, every student should work with every other classmate. An elementary setting allows students to be in several different learning groups during the day. Our best advice is to allow groups to remain stable long enough for them to be successful. Breaking up groups that are having trouble functioning effectively is often counterproductive as the students do not learn the skills they need to resolve problems in collaborating with each other.

There is merit in having students work with everyone in their class during a semester or school year. Building a strong positive feeling of collaboration across an entire class and giving students opportunities to practice the skills needed to begin new groups can add much to a school year. **Never underestimate the power of heterogeneous cooperative learning groups in promoting high quality, rich, and involved learning.**

## Arranging the Room

How the teacher arranges the room is a symbolic message of what is appropriate behavior and it can facilitate the learning groups within the classroom. Members of a learning group should sit close enough to each other that they can share materials, maintain eye contact with all group members, and talk to each other quietly without disrupting the other learning groups.  Circles are usually best.  The teacher should have a clear access lane to every group.  Common mistakes that teachers make in arranging a room are to (1) place students at a rectangular table where they cannot have eye contact with all the other members or (2) move several desks together, which may place students too far apart to communicate quietly with each other and share materials.  Within each learning group students need to be able to see all relevant task materials, see each other, converse with each other without raising their voices, and exchange ideas and materials in a comfortable atmosphere.  The groups need to be far enough apart so that they do not interfere with each other's learning.  "Knee-to-knee and eye-to-eye"--the closer the better.

# Planning the Instructional Materials to Promote Interdependence

Materials need to be distributed among group members so that all members participate and achieve.  When a group is mature and experienced and group members have a high level of collaborative skills, the teacher may not have to arrange materials in any specific way.  When a group is new or when members are not very skilled, however, teachers may wish to distribute materials in carefully planned ways to communicate that the assignment is to be a joint (not an individual) effort and that the students are in a "sink or swim together" learning situation.  Three of the ways of doing so are:

1. **Materials Interdependence**: Give only one copy of the materials to the group.  The students will then have to work together in order to be successful.  This is especially effective the first few times the group meets.  After students are accustomed to collaborating with each other, teachers will wish each student to have an individual copy of the materials.

2. **Information Interdependence**: Group members may each be given different books or resource materials to be synthesized. Or the materials may be arranged like a jigsaw puzzle so that each student has part of the materials needed to complete the task. Such procedures require that every member participate in order for the group to be successful.

3. **Interdependence from Outside Enemies**: Materials may be structured into a tournament format with intergroup competition as the basis to promote a perception of interdependence among group members. Such a procedure was introduced by Devries and Edwards (1973). In the teams-games-tournament format students are divided into heterogeneous cooperative learning teams to prepare members for a tournament in which they compete with the other teams. During the intergroup competition the students individually compete against members of about the same ability level from other teams. The team whose members do the best in the competition is pronounced the winner by the teacher.

All of these procedures may not be needed simultaneously. They are alternative methods of ensuring that students perceive that they are involved in a "sink or swim together" learning situation and behave collaboratively.

# Assigning Roles to Ensure Interdependence

Positive interdependence may also be arranged through the assignment of complementary and interconnected roles to group members. Each group member is assigned a responsibility that the group needs to work effectively. Such roles include a **summarizer** (who restates the group's major conclusions or answers), a **checker** (who ensures that all group members can explicitly explain how to arrive at an answer or conclusion), an **accuracy coach** (who corrects any mistakes in another member's explanations or summaries), a **relater/elaboration seeker** (who asks members to relate current concepts and strategies to material studied previously), a **researcher-runner** (who gets needed materials for the group and communicates with the other learning groups and the teacher), a **recorder** to write down the group's decisions and edit the group's report, an **encourager** to reinforce members' contributions, and an **observer** to keep track of how well the group is collaborating. Assigning such roles is an effective method of teaching students collaborative skills and fostering positive interdependence.

# Explaining the Academic Task

Teachers explain the academic task so that students are clear about the assignment and understand the objectives of the lesson. Direct teaching of concepts, principles, and strategies may take place at this point. Teachers may wish to answer any questions students have about the concepts or facts they are to learn or apply in the lesson. Teachers need to consider several aspects of explaining an academic assignment to students:

1. **Set the task so that students are clear about the assignment.** Most teachers have considerable practice with this already. Instructions that are clear and specific are crucial in warding off student frustration. One advantage of cooperative learning groups is that they can handle more ambiguous tasks (when they are appropriate) than can students working alone. In cooperative learning groups students who do not understand what they are to do will ask their group for clarification before asking the teacher.

2. **Explain the objectives of the lesson and relate the concepts and information to be studied to students' past experience and learning to ensure maximum transfer and retention.** Explaining the intended outcomes of the lesson increases the likelihood that students will focus on the relevant concepts and information throughout the lesson.

3. **Define relevant concepts, explain procedures students should follow, and give examples to help students understand what they are to learn and do in completing the assignment.** To promote positive transfer of learning, point out the critical elements that separate this lesson from past learnings.

4. **Ask the class specific questions to check the students' understanding of the assignment.** Such questioning ensures thorough two-way communication, that the assignment has been given effectively, and that the students are ready to begin completing it.

# Structuring Positive Goal Interdependence

Communicate to students that they have a group goal and must work collaboratively. We cannot overemphasize the importance of communicating to students that they are in a "sink or swim together" learning situation. In a cooperative learning group students are responsible for learning the assigned material, making sure that all other group members learn the assigned material, and making sure that all other class members successfully learn the assigned material, in that order. Teachers can do this in several ways.

1. **Ask the group to produce a single product, report, or paper.** Each group member should sign the paper to indicate that he or she agrees with the answers and can explain why the answers are appropriate. Each student must know the material. When a group is producing only one product it is especially important to stress individual accountability. Teachers may pick a student at random from each group to explain the rationale for their answers.

2. **Provide group rewards**. Bonus points and a total group score are ways to give students the "sink or swim together" message. An example is a spelling group where

members work with each other during the week to make sure that all members learn their words correctly. They then take the test individually and are rewarded on the basis of the total number of words spelled correctly by all group members. Math lessons can be structured so that students work in cooperative learning groups, take a test individually, receive their individual score, and be given bonus points on the basis of how many group members reach a preset level of excellence. Some teachers have students work in cooperative learning groups, give individual tests, give students individual grades on the basis of their scores, and then reward groups where all members reach a preset criteria of excellence with free-time or extra recess.

**Positive interdependence creates peer encouragement and support for learning.** Such positive peer pressure influences underachieving students to become academically involved. Members of cooperative learning groups should give interrelated messages, "Do your work--we're counting on you!" and "How can I help you to do better?"

# Structuring Individual Accountability

The purpose of a cooperative group is to maximize the learning of each member. A group is not truly cooperative if members are "slackers" who let others do all the work. To ensure that all members learn and that groups know which members to provide with encouragement and help, teachers need to assess frequently the level of performance of each group member. Practice tests, randomly selecting members to explain answers, having members edit each other's work, teach what they know to someone else, use what they have learned on a different problem, and randomly picking one paper from the group to grade, are ways to structure individual accountability.

# Structuring Intergroup Cooperation

The positive outcomes found within a cooperative learning group can be extended throughout a whole class by structuring intergroup cooperation. Bonus points may be given if all members of a class reach a preset criteria of excellence. When a group finishes its work, the teacher should encourage the members to go help other groups complete the assignment.

# Explaining Criteria for Success

Evaluation within cooperatively structured lessons needs to be criterion-referenced. Criterion must be established for acceptable work (rather than grading on a curve). Thus, at the beginning of the lesson teachers should clearly explain the criterion by which the students' work will be evaluated. The criterion for success must be structured so that students may reach it without penalizing other students and so that groups may reach it without penalizing other groups. For some learning groups all members can be working to reach the same criterion. For other learning groups different members may be evaluated according to different criteria. The criterion should be tailored to be challenging and realistic for each individual group member. In a spelling group, for example, some members may not be able to learn as many as 20 words and their number can be reduced accordingly. **Teachers may structure a second level of cooperation by not only keeping track of how well each group and its members are performing, but also by setting criterion for the whole class to reach.** Thus, the number of words the total class spells correctly can be recorded from week to week with an appropriate criterion being set to promote class-wide collaboration and encouragement. Criteria are important to give students information about what "doing well" is on assigned tasks, but they do not always have to be as formal as counting the number correct. On some assignments, simply completing the task may be adequate for a criterion. Or simply doing better this week than one did last week may be set as a criterion of excellence.

# Specifying Desired Behaviors

The word **cooperation** has many different connotations and uses. Teachers will need to define cooperation operationally by specifying the behaviors that are appropriate and desirable within the learning groups. There are beginning behaviors, such as "stay with your group and do not wander around the room," "use quiet voices," "take turns," and "use each other's names." When groups begin to function effectively, expected behaviors may include:

1. Having each member explain how to get the answer.

2. Asking each member to relate what is being learned to previous learnings.

3. Checking to make sure everyone in the group understands the material and agrees with the answers.

4. Encouraging everyone to participate.

5. Listening accurately to what other group members are saying.

6. Not changing your mind unless you are logically persuaded (majority rule does not promote learning).

7. Criticizing ideas, not people.

Teachers should not make the list of expected behaviors too long. One or two behaviors to emphasize for a few lessons is enough. Students need to know what behavior is appropriate and desirable within a cooperative learning group, but they should not be subjected to information overload.

# Monitoring Students' Behavior

The teacher's job begins in earnest when the cooperative learning groups start working. Resist that urge to go get a cup of coffee or grade some papers. Just because the teacher instructs students to cooperate and places them in learning groups does not mean that they will always do so. So, much of the teacher's time in cooperative learning situations should be spent observing group members in order to see what problems they are having in completing the assignment and in working collaboratively. A variety of observation instruments and procedures that can be used for these purposes can be found in Johnson and F. Johnson (1987), Johnson, Johnson, and Holubec (1987).

Whenever possible, teachers should use a formal observation sheet where they count the number of times they observe appropriate behaviors being used by students. The more concrete the data, the more useful it is to the teacher and to students. Teachers should not try to count too many different behaviors at one time, especially when they first start formal observation. At first they may want just to keep track of who talks in each group to get a participation pattern for the groups. We have a chapter describing systematic observation of cooperative groups in **Learning Together and Alone** (1987a) and our current list of behaviors (though rather long) includes: contributing ideas, asking questions, expressing feelings, active listening, expressing support and acceptance (toward ideas), expressing warmth and liking (toward group members and group), encouraging all members to participate, summarizing, checking for understanding, relieving tension by joking, and giving direction to group's work. All the behaviors we look for are positive behaviors which are to be praised when they are appropriately present and are a cause for discussion when they are missing. It is also a good idea for the teacher to collect notes on specific student behaviors so that the frequency data is extended. Especially useful are skillful interchanges that can be shared with students later as objective praise and perhaps with parents in conferences or telephone conversations.

Student observers can be used to get even more extensive data on each group's functioning. For very young students the system must be kept very simple, perhaps only "Who talks?" Many teachers have had good success with student observers, even in kindergarten. One of the more important things to do is for the teacher to make sure that the class is given adequate instructions (and perhaps practice) on gathering the observation data and sharing it with the group. The observer is in the best position to learn about the skills of working in a group. We can remember one first grade teacher who had a student who talked all the time (even to himself while working alone). He tended to dominate any group he was in. When she introduced student observers to the class she made him an observer. One important rule for observers was not to interfere in the task but to gather data without talking. He was gathering data on who talks and he did a good job, noticing that one student had done quite a bit of talking in the group while another had talked very little. The next day when he was a group member, and there was another observer, he was seen starting to talk, clamping his hand over his mouth and glancing at the observer. He knew what was being observed for and he didn't want to be the only one with marks. The teacher said he may have listened for the first time in the year. So the observer often benefits in learning about group skills.

When teachers are worried about losing the lesson content (observers, however, often know quite a bit about the lesson) then they can have the group as a last review take the observer through the material and see if they can get her signature on the paper as well. Often important changes are made during this review.

It is not necessary to use student observers all the time and we would not recommend their use until cooperative learning groups are used a few times. It is enough for teachers just to structure the groups to be cooperative in the beginning without having to worry about structuring student observers, too. Whether student observers are used or not, however, teachers should always do some observing and spend some time monitoring the groups. Sometimes a simple checklist is helpful in addition to a sys-

tematic observation form. Some questions to ask on the checklist might be:

1. Do students understand the task?

2. Have students accepted the positive interdependence and
   the individual accountability?

3. Are students working toward the criteria, and are those
   criteria for success appropriate?

4. Are students practicing the specified behaviors, or not?

# Providing Task Assistance

In monitoring the groups as they work, teachers will wish to
clarify instructions, review important procedures and strategies
for completing the assignment, answer questions, and teach task
skills as necessary. In discussing the concepts and information
to be learned, teachers will wish to use the language or terms
relevant to the learning. Instead of saying, "Yes, that is right,"
teachers will wish to say something more specific to the assignment, such as, "Yes, that is one way to find the main idea of a
paragraph." The use of the more specific statement reinforces
the desired learning and promotes positive transfer by helping
the students associate a term with their learning.

# Intervening to Teach Collaborative Skills

While monitoring the learning groups teachers will also find students who do not have the necessary collaborative skills and
groups where problems in collaborating have arisen. **In these
cases the teacher will wish to intervene to suggest more effective procedures for working together and more effective
behaviors for students to engage in.** Teachers may also wish
to intervene and reinforce particularly effective and skillful be-

haviors that they notice. At times the teacher becomes a consultant to a group in order to help it function more effectively. When it is obvious that group members lack certain social skills they need in order to cooperate with each other, the teacher will want to intervene in order to help the members learn the collaborative skills. The social skills required for productive group work, along with activities that may be used in teaching them, are covered in Johnson and F. Johnson (1987) and Johnson (1986, 1987).

**Teachers should not intervene any more than is absolutely necessary in the groups.** Most of us as teachers are geared to jumping in and solving problems for students to get them back on track. With a little patience we would find that cooperative groups can often work their way through their own problems (task and maintenance) and acquire not only a solution, but also a method of solving similar problems in the future. Choosing when to intervene and when not to is part of the art of teaching and with some restraint, teachers can usually trust their intuition. Even when intervening, teachers can turn the problem back to the group to solve. Many teachers intervene in a group by having members set aside their task, pointing out the problem, and asking the group to come up with an adequate solution. (The last thing teachers want to happen is for the students to learn to come running to the teacher with every problem.)

In one third grade class, the teacher noticed when passing out papers that one student was sitting back away from the other three. A moment later the teacher glanced over and only three students were sitting where four were a moment before. As she watched, the three students came marching over to her and complained that Johnny was under the table and wouldn't come out. "Make him come out!" they insisted (the teacher's role: police-officer, judge, and executioner). The teacher told them that Johnny was a member of their group and asked what they had tried to solve their problem. "Tried?" the puzzled reply. "Yes, have you asked him to come out?" the teacher suggested. The group marched back and the teacher continued passing out papers to groups. A moment later the teacher glanced over to their table and saw no heads above the table (which is one way to solve the problem). After a few more minutes, four heads came struggling out from under the table and the group (including Johnny) went back to work with great energy. We don't know what happened under that table, but whatever it was, it was effective. What makes this story even more interesting is that the group received a 100 percent on the paper and later, when the teacher was standing by Johnny's desk, she noticed he had the paper clutched in his hand. The group had given Johnny the paper and he was taking it home. He confided to the teacher that this was the first time he could ever remember earning a 100 percent on anything in school. (If that was your record, you might slip under a few tables yourself.)

**The best time to teach cooperative skills is when the students need them.** Intervening should leave a cooperative learning group with new skills that will be useful in the future. It is important that the cooperative skills be taught in the context of the class where they are going to be used, or are practiced in that setting, because transfer of skill learning from one situation to another cannot be assumed. **Students learn about cooperative skills when they are taught them, and learn cooperative skills when applying them in the midst of science, math, or English.** The good news about cooperative skills is that they are taught and learned like any other skill. At a minimum:

1. **Students need to recognize the need for the skill.**

2. **The skill must be defined clearly and specifically including what students should say when engaging in the skill.**

3. **The practice of the skill must be encouraged.** Sometimes just the teacher standing there with a clipboard and pencil will be enough to promote student enactment of the skill.

4. **Students should have the time and procedures for discussing how well they are using the skills.** Students should persevere in the practice until the skill is appropriately internalized. We never drop a skill, we only add on.

For older students (upper elementary school and above) the skills have been well described in **Joining Together** (Johnson & F. Johnson, 1987) and **Reaching Out** (Johnson, 1990). For younger students, teachers may need to revise and rename cooperative skills. Some primary teachers use symbols like traffic signs with a "green light" to represent encouraging participation, a "stop sign" to mean time to summarize, and "slippery when wet" to mean "say that over again, I didn't quite understand." Sometimes a more mechanistic structure is beneficial for young students. In one first grade class the teacher had a number of students who liked to take over the group and dominate. One day in frustration, she formed groups and handed out to each group member five poker chips with a different color for each group member. The students were instructed to place a chip in the box every time they spoke while they worked on the worksheet. When a student had "spent" all his or her chips, he or she could not speak. When all the chips were in the box, they could get their five colored chips back and start again. There were several surprised students when their five chips were the only chips in the box! Teachers only have to use this once or twice to get the message across (although first grade students can get addicted to chips, so watch out). This technique was later used in a monthly principals' meeting. As the principals came in, each was handed several colored strips of paper. When they spoke..

Teaching your students how to work together effectively is a necessary part of implementing cooperative learning into your classroom. We would recommend that only a few skills be taught in one semester. Most of the curriculum programs with cooperative learning groups written into them feature about five to eight cooperative skills for a year.

## Providing Closure to the Lesson

At the end of the lesson students should be able to summarize what they have learned and to understand where they will use it in future lessons. Teachers may wish to summarize the major points in the lesson, ask students to recall ideas or give samples, and answer any final questions students have.

# Evaluating the Quality and Quantity of Students' Learning

The product required from the lesson may be a report, a single set of answers that all members of the group agree to, the average of individual examination scores, or the number of group members reaching a specific criterion. Whatever the measure, the learning of group members needs to be evaluated by a criterion-referenced system. The procedures for setting up and using such an evaluation system are given in Johnson and Johnson (1987a). Besides assessing students on how well they learn the assigned concepts and information, group members should also receive feedback on how effectively they collaborated. Some teachers give two grades, one for achievement and one for collaborative behavior.

# Assessing How Well the Group Functioned

An old observational rule is, **if you observe, you must process your observations with the group.** Even if class time is limited, some time should be spent talking about how well the groups functioned today, what things were done well, and what things could be improved. Each learning group may have its own observer and spend time discussing how effectively members are working together. Teachers may also wish to spend some time in **whole-class processing** where they give the class feedback and have students share incidents that occurred in their groups and how they were solved. Names do not need to be used, but the feedback should be as specific as possible.

Discussing group functioning is essential. A common teaching error is to provide too brief a time for students to process the quality of their collaboration. Students do not learn from experiences that they do not reflect on. If the learning groups are to function better tomorrow than they did today, members must receive feedback, reflect on how their actions may be more effective, and plan how to be even more skillful during the next group session.

**Every small group has two primary goals: (1) to accomplish the task successfully, and (2) to build and maintain constructive relationships in good working order for the next task.** Learning groups are often exclusively task oriented and ignore the importance of maintaining effective working relationships among members. Group sessions should be enjoyable, lively, and pleasant experiences. If no one is having fun, something is wrong. Problems in collaborating should be brought up and solved and there should be a continuing emphasis on improving the effectiveness of the group members in collaborating with each other.

Often during the "working" part of the class period, students will be very task-oriented and the "maintenance" of the group may suffer. During the processing time, however, the emphasis is on maintenance of the group and the students leave the room ready for (a better?) tomorrow. If no processing is done, teachers may find the group's functioning decaying and important relationship issues left undiscussed. Processing may not need to occur each day in depth, but it should happen often. **Processing the functioning of the group needs to be taken as seriously as accomplishing the task.** The two are very much related. Teachers often have students turn in a "process sheet" along with the paper from the task assignment.

**Group processing provides a structure for group members to hold each other accountable for being responsible and skillful group members.** In order to contribute to each other's learning, group members need to attend class, be prepared (i.e., have done the necessary homework), and contribute to the group's work. A student's absenteeism and lack of preparation often demoralizes other members. Productive group work requires members to be present and prepared, and there should be some peer accountability to be so. When groups "process," they discuss any member actions that need to be improved in order for everyone's learning to be maximized.

**Groups new to processing often need an agenda**, including specific questions each group member must address. Inex-perienced groups tend to say, "We did fine. Right? Right!" and not deal with any real issues. A simple agenda could be to have each group name two things they did well (and document them) and one thing they need to be even better at, or would like to work harder on.

# Structuring Academic Controversies

Within cooperative groups students often disagree as to what answers to assignments should be and how the group should function in order to maximize members' learning. Conflict is an inherent part of learning as old conclusions and conceptions are challenged and modified to take into account new information and broader perspectives. **Controversy** is a type of academic conflict that exists when one student's ideas, information, con-clusions, theories, and opinions are incompatible with those of another, and the two seek to reach an agreement. When stu-dents become experienced in working cooperatively, and when teachers wish to increase students' emotional involvement in learning and motivation to achieve, teachers may structure con-troversy into cooperative learning groups by structuring five phases (Johnson & Johnson, 1987b; Johnson, Johnson, & Smith, 1986):

1. Assign students to groups of four, then divide the group into two pairs. One pair is given the pro position and the other pair is given the con position on an issue being studied. Each pair prepares their position.

2. Each pair presents its position to the other pair.

3. Students argue the two positions.

4. Pairs reverse perspectives and argue the opposing position.

5. Groups of four reach a decision and come to a consensus on a position that is supported by facts and logic and can be defended by each group member.

# Conclusions

These eighteen aspects of structuring learning situations cooperatively blend together to make effective, cooperative learning groups a reality in the classroom. They may be used in any subject area with any age student. One of the things we have been told many times by teachers who have mastered these strategies and integrated cooperative learning groups into their teaching is, "Don't say it is easy!" We know it's not. It can take years to become an expert. There is a lot of pressure to teach like everyone else, to have students learn alone, and not let students look at each other's papers. Students will not be accustomed to working together and are likely to have a competitive orientation. You may wish to start small by taking one subject area or one class and use cooperative learning until you feel comfortable, and then expand into other subject areas or other classes. In order to implement cooperative learning successfully, you will need to teach students the interpersonal and small group skills required to collaborate, structure and orchestrate intellectual inquiry within learning groups, and form collaborative relations with other others. **Implementing cooperative learning in your classroom is not easy, but it is worth the effort.**

# Chapter 4

# Creating Positive Interdependence

## Key To Cooperation: We Instead Of Me

*"United we stand, divided we fall."*

Watchword of the American Revolution

Author William Manchester wrote several years ago in Life Magazine about revisiting Sugar Loaf Hill in Okinawa, where 34 years before he had fought as a Marine. He describes how he had been wounded, sent to a hospital and, in violation of orders, escaped from the hospital to rejoin his Army unit at the front. Doing so meant almost certain death. "Why did I do it?" he wondered. The answer lies in the power of positive interdependence.

**Positive interdependence** is the perception that you are linked with others in a way so that you cannot succeed unless they do (and vice versa), that is, their work benefits you and your work benefits them. It promotes a situation in which individuals work together in small groups to maximize the learning of all members. In such a situation individuals perceive:

1. Group members are striving for **mutual benefit** so that all members of the group will gain. There is recognition that what helps other group members benefits you and what promotes your productivity benefits the other group members. Each member invests time and energy into helping groupmates, which then pays dividends and capital gains when groupmates score high on tests and reciprocate the helping.

2. Group members share a **common fate** where they all gain or lose on the basis of their overall performance.

3. The performance of group members is **mutually caused**. Within a cooperative learning group, you are **responsible** for giving the help and assistance other members need to be productive and **obligated** to the other members for the support and assistance they gave to you. Each member is instrumental in the productivity of each other member. Your productivity, therefore, is perceived to be caused by (a) your own efforts and abilities and (b) the efforts and abilities of the other group members, and the performance of the other group members is perceived to be due partially to your encouragement and facilitation. The mutual responsibility and mutual obligation inherent in the mutual causation within cooperative learning groups results in a **mutual investment** by members in each other.

4. There is a **shared identity** based on group membership. Besides being a separate individual, you are a member of a team. The shared identity binds members together emotionally.

5. The **self-efficacy** of members is increased through the empowerment inherent in the joint efforts. Being part of a cooperative learning group increases students' confidence that if they exert effort, they will be successful. Cooperative groups empower their members to act by making them feel strong, capable, and committed. **Being part of a team effort changes feelings of "I can't do it" to "We can do it."** Success that is impossible for one person to achieve is attainable within a cooperative group. A student may believe, "I can't do algebra, it's too hard," until two other students say, "Stick with us; we'll get you through algebra with at least a 'B.'" The student then tends to believe, "We can do algebra."

6. There are **joint celebrations** based on (a) mutual respect and appreciation for the efforts of group members and (b) the group's success. Being part of a team effort results in

feelings of (a) camaraderie, belonging, and pride and (b) success. Feelings of success are shared and pride is taken in others' accomplishments as well as one's own.

# Barriers To Positive Interdependence: The Delusion Of Individualism

The feelings and commitment that drove William Manchester to risk his life to help protect his comrads do not automatically appear when students are placed in learning groups. There are barriers to positive interdependence. Among many current high school and college students, their own pleasures and pains, successes and failures, occupy center stage in their lives (Conger, 1988; Seligman, 1988). Each person tends to focus on gratifying his or her own ends without concern for others. Over the past 20 years, self-interest has become more important than commitment to community or country. Young adults have turned away from careers of public service to careers of self-service. Many young adults have a **delusion of individualism** , believing that (1) they are separate and apart from all other individuals and, therefore, (2) others' frustration, unhappiness, hunger, despair, and misery have no significant bearing on their own well-being. With the increase in the past two decades in adolescents' and youth's concern for personal well-being, there has been a corresponding diminished concern for the welfare of others (particularly the less advantaged) and of society itself (Astin, Green, & Korn, 1987; Astin, Green, Korn, & Schalit, 1986).

The self is a very poor site for finding meaning. Hope does not spring from competition. Meaning does not surface in individualistic efforts aimed at benefiting no one but yourself. Empowerment does not come from isolation. Purpose does not grow from egocentric focus on own material gain. Without involvement in interdependent efforts and the resulting concern for others, it is not possible to realize oneself except in the most superficial sense. Contributing to the well-being of others within an interdependent effort provides meaning and purpose to life.

# Power Of Positive Interdependence

For an individual, piloting a Boeing 747 is impossible. For the three-person crew, it is straightforward. The crew, furthermore, does not work in isolation. Large numbers of mechanics, service personnel, cabin attendants, air traffic controllers, pilot educators (who keep crew members abreast of the latest developments and sharp in their responses to problem situations), and many others are necessary to the flying of the plane. From the demands of repairing a flat tire on a dark highway ("You hold the light while I...") to the complex requirements of flying a modern passenger jet, teamwork is the most frequent human response to the challenges of coping with otherwise impossible tasks.

Within the real world, positive interdependence is pervasive on many levels. Individuals join together into a group that is structured around a mutual goal. The group fits into the larger mosaic of groups working toward a larger goal. Those groups also form a mosaic working toward even a larger superordinate goal. Thus, there are individuals who work within teams that work within departments that work within divisions that work within organizations that work within a societal economic system that works within the global economic system.

Life in the real world is characterized by layers of positive interdependence that stretch from the interpersonal to the international. Life in schools is dominated by competitive and individualistic activities that ignore the importance of positive interdependence. It is time for classrooms to become more realistic.

## Positive Interdependence In The Classroom

When positive interdependence is carefully structured, you tend to see students:

    1. Putting their heads close together over their work.

2. Talking about the work.

3. Drilling each other on the material being learned.

4. Sharing answers and materials.

5. Encouraging each other to learn.

When positive interdependence is **not** carefully structured, you may see students:

1. Leaving their group impulsively.

2. Talking about topics other than the work.

3. Doing their own work while ignoring other students.

4. Not sharing answers or materials.

5. Not checking to see if others have learned the material.

To implement cooperative learning, you need to understand the types of positive interdependence and have specific strategies for implementing each one. In doing so you should follow the general procedure of:

1. **Structuring** positive goal interdependence within a lesson and supplementing it with a number of other types of positive interdependence.

2. **Informing** students of the types of positive interdependence present in the lesson and emphasize that they "sink or swim together."

3. **Monitoring** students' actions to ensure that they truly believe that they are responsible for each other's learning as well as their own.

4. Have groups **process** the extent to which they really believed that they were responsible for each other's learning and success.

With modifying a few words, this sequence may be called **STOP** (**S**tructure, **T**ell, **O**bserve, **P**rocess).

# Types Of Positive Interdependence

Since at first most students (especially older ones) do not automatically care about their groupmates, positive interdependence must be consciously and clearly structured by the teacher. Cooperative efforts begin with the establishment of mutual goals, around which the actions of each group member are organized. To ensure that the group works productively and exerts considerable effort toward accomplishing the mutual goal, members with different resources are assigned roles and given a task that requires coordination of efforts. They are also given a team identity and a setting in which to work. To highlight the importance of the goal, the long-term implications of success are spelled out. Threats to team success are identified. An identity based on the importance of the goal is established. Finally, the rewards of success are made salient to induce members to join in the joint effort.

## Positive Goal Interdependence 1: Learning Goals

The first step in structuring positive interdependence within a cooperative learning group is to set a mutual goal that establishes that members are responsible for each other's learning and success as well as their own. **Positive goal interdependence** exists when students perceive that they can achieve their learning goals if, and only if, all other members of their group also attain their goals. Members of a learning group have a mutual set of goals that they all are striving to accomplish. Success depends on all members reaching the goal. The goal might be that all group members understand how to do long division with remainders or that all group members be able to analyze the plot of **Hamlet**. All cooperative lessons need to include positive goal interdependence. Other types of positive interdependence support and supplement the effects of positive goal interdependence. Ways of structuring positive goal interdependence include the following:

1. **Teachers explain that the group goal is to ensure that all members achieve a prescribed mastery level on the assigned material.** This means each group member has two responsibilities: (a) learn and (b) ensure that all other group members learn. Teachers may wish to say, "One answer from the three of you, everyone has to agree, and everyone has to be able to explain how to solve the problem or complete the assignment." Teachers may establish the prescribed mastery level as (a) individual levels of performance that each group member must achieve in order for the group as a whole to be successful (the group goal is for each member to demonstrate 90 percent mastery on a curriculum unit) or (b) improvement scores (the group goal is to ensure that all members do better this week than they did last week).

2. **Teachers "enlarge the shadow of the future" by:**

   a. Showing that the long-term benefits of cooperation outweigh the short-term benefits of taking advantage of the other group members or of not cooperating. Teachers may wish to demonstrate that sharing the work and helping each other learn is more productive and fun than competing or working alone. The long-term vision must be more compelling than the temptation of short-term personal advantage.

   b. Highlighting the facts that interactions among group members will be frequent and the relationships among team members will be durable. The shadow of the future looms largest when interactions among students are frequent and durable. **Durability** promotes cooperative efforts because it makes interpersonal relationships long lasting. It ensures that students will not easily forget how they have treated, and been treated by, each other. **Frequency** promotes stability by making the consequences of today's actions more salient for tomorrow's work. When students realize they will work with each other frequently and for a long period of time, they see the need to be cooperative and supportive in current dealings with each other.

3. **Teachers add the scores of all group members to determine an overall group score.** This score is compared with the preset criterion of excellence. Teachers may wish to say, "The goal of each triad is to reach a total group score of 135 out of 150 potential correct answers." Since there are 50 questions on the test, each member needs to get at least 45 correct on the test. To highlight the goal of maximizing the total group score teachers may wish to keep a group progress chart. Total group scores may be plotted each day or each week. Students are then responsible for raising their own and their groupmates' performances in order to show progress on the group chart.

4. **Teachers choose randomly the worksheet, report, or theme of one group member to be evaluated.** This means that members are responsible for reading and correcting each other's work to ensure that it is 100 percent correct before the teacher selects one representative paper on which to evaluate the group. Variations include randomly selecting one member to demonstrate mastery of a concept, translate a sentence in a foreign language class, or take the test for the group. Since this is a procedure to ensure each individual group member is accountable for learning the assigned material, it demonstrates that there is an intimate relationship between goal interdependence and individual accountability. **Individual accountability** is the measurement of whether or not each group member has achieved the group's goal. Individual accountability cannot exist unless goal interdependence has been previously established.

5. **Teachers request one product** (such as a report, theme, presentation, or answer sheet) from the group that is signed by all members. Signatures indicate that each member was active in creating the product, agrees with it, and can rationally defend its content. A variation on this procedure is to implement a rule that no group member

receives credit for doing homework until all group members have handed in the homework assignment. Groups
may be responsible for writing a newsletter or making a
presentation, and each member does not receive credit unless all group members contribute an article to the newsletter or make part of the presentation. This may be
extended into intergroup cooperation by having the class
produce a newspaper in which each group has contributed a part (which in turn must contain work by each individual member), or by having the class give a
Renaissance Day in which each group must make a
presentation (which in turn must include all members).

Students will contribute more energy and effort to meaningful
goals than to trivial ones. Being responsible for others' learning
as well as for one's own gives cooperative efforts a meaning that
is not found in competitive and individualistic learning situations.
In cooperative learning situations, the efforts of each group member contribute not only to their own success, but also to the success of groupmates. When there is meaning to what they do,
ordinary people exert extraordinary effort. It is positive goal interdependence that gives meaning to the efforts of group members.

## Positive Goal Interdependence 2: Outside Enemy Interdependence

The goal of a learning group may be to learn more than other
groups in order to win a competition. **Positive outside enemy
interdependence** exists when groups are placed in competition
with each other. Group members then feel interdependent as
they strive to beat the other groups. A procedure we like is
having students compete with the score made by last years'
class or the total class score made last week. A teacher might
say, "Last year's class made a total score of 647 on this test. Can
you do better? Sure you can." Such competition reduces the
negative behavior that often accompanies competing against
other groups in the same class.

## Positive Goal Interdependence 3: Fantasy Interdependence

The goals that learning groups strive to achieve do not have to be real. **Positive fantasy interdependence** exists when students imagine that they are in an emergency situation (such as surviving a ship wreak) or must deal with problems (such as ending air pollution in the world) that are compelling but unreal. A teacher may say, "You are the **world's leading scientists**. Your challenge is to save the world by finding the answers to these difficult and mystifying equations!" We like to tell students that they are **word detectives** who must look for a certain word in a reading assignment and describe how it is used by the author. Students may also be **character detectives** who analyze a character in a story or play.

## Positive Reward / Celebration Interdependence

In order for students to look forward to working in cooperative groups, and enjoy doing so, they must feel that (1) their efforts are appreciated and (2) they are respected as an individual. Long-term commitment to achieve is largely based on feeling recognized and respected for what one is doing. Thus, students' efforts to learn and promote each other's learning need to be (1) observed, (2) recognized, and (3) celebrated. The celebration of individual efforts and group success involves structuring reward interdependence.

**Positive reward interdependence** exists when each group member receives the same reward for completing the assignment. A joint reward is given for successful group work. Everyone is rewarded or no one is rewarded. An example of reward interdependence is when every group member receives 5 bonus points (or 15 extra recess minutes) when all group members get 90 percent correct on a test. The rewards should be attractive to students, inexpensive, and consistent with your philosophy of teaching. It is important that groups that do not reach the criteria do not receive the reward. The rewards, furthermore, should probably be removed as soon as the intrinsic motivation inherent

| Errors | Effective Practices |
|---|---|
| Not knowing if students are helping each other | Constant monitoring of groups to make helping visible |
| Informing teachers | Swapping "good news" among group members |
| Only recognition from teacher is important | Recognition and respect from peers |
| Recognizing only the few class superstars | Recognizing almost everyone |
| Trivializing rewards by rewarding students for anything | Rewarding only completed valuable actions |

in cooperative learning groups becomes apparent. You will know when this happens when students pressure you to let them work in groups. Ways of structuring positive reward interdependence include the following:

1. Teachers give bonus points that are added to all members' academic scores when everyone in the group achieves up to criterion.

2. Teachers give nonacademic rewards (such as extra free time, extra recess time, stickers, stars, or food) when all group members reach criteria on an academic task.

3. Teachers give teacher praise (i.e., social rewards) for the group as a whole when all group members reach criteria.

4. Teachers give a single group grade for the combined efforts of group members. This should be cautiously done until all students (and parents) are very familiar with cooperative learning.

5. Group members swapping "good news" about each other's efforts to promote each other's learning and celebrating their joint success. Group members and teachers should:

a. Seek out valuable, completed actions by group members in completing assignments and helping group-mates complete assignments.

b. Honor the actions with all sorts of positive recognition. In doing so, interpersonal recognition rather than formal evaluation should be emphasized. Supportive, encouraging, and caring interaction among team members is the key. **There is nothing more motivating to students than having groupmates cheering them on and jointly celebrating their successes.**

## Positive Resource Interdependence

**Positive resource interdependence** exists when each member has only a portion of the information, resources, or materials necessary for the task to be completed and members' resources have to be combined in order for the group to achieve its goal. Thus, the resources of each group member are needed if the task is to be completed. Ways of structuring positive resource interdependence include the following:

1. The teacher limiting the resources given to the group. Only one pencil, for example, may be given to a group of three students. Other resources that can be limited include textbooks, answer sheets, scissors, dictionaries, maps, typewriters, computers, and periodic charts of elements.

2. The teacher jigsawing materials so that each member has part of a set of materials. Materials that can be jigsawed include vocabulary words, lines of a poem, letters of a word, sentences of a paragraph to be sequenced, words for a sentence, pictures, definitions, puzzle pieces, problems, parts of directions, resource materials, lab equipment, parts of a map, art supplies, ingredients for cooking, and sections of a report. One social studies teacher gave each member of his cooperative learning groups a different social studies text and then gave assignments requiring stu-

dents to share what each text had to say about the issue. Each member of a group may be given one sentence of a paragraph and the group is given the task of sequencing the sentences. A group could be given the assignment of writing a biography of Abe Lincoln and information on Lincoln's childhood given to one member, information on Lincoln's early political career given to another, information on Lincoln as president given to a third, and information on Lincoln's assassination given to the fourth member. A different type of jigsaw is created when the assignment is to make a collage and one member has the paste, another has the scissors, and a third has the magazines.

3. The teacher giving students a writing assignment with the stipulation that each member must offer a sentence in each paragraph, contribute an article to a newsletter, write a paragraph or an essay, or do a chapter in a "book."

## Positive Task Interdependence

**Positive task interdependence** exists when a division of labor is created so that the actions of one group member have to be completed if the next team member is to complete his or her responsibilities. Dividing an overall task into subunits that must be performed **in a set order** is an example of task interdependence. This "factory-line" model exists when one student is responsible for obtaining swamp-water, another is responsible for making slides, another is responsible for viewing the slides through a microscope, and the fourth member is responsible for writing down the organisms found in the swamp- water. Another example is a "chain reaction" where a student named Bill learns a concept and then is responsible for teaching it to another student named Jane, and the test score received by Jane is given to Bill. While task interdependence is closely related to resource interdependence, it is used much less frequently as not very many academic tasks lend themselves to such a "lock-step" division-of-labor.

## Positive Role Interdependence

**Positive role interdependence** exists when each member is assigned complementary and interconnected roles that specify responsibilities that the group needs in order to complete a joint task. Any of the skills discussed in Chapter 5 may be used. Usually the roles are rotated daily so that each student obtains considerable experience in each role. Some roles to get you started are:

**Reader**: Reads the group's material out loud to the group, carefully and with expression, so that group members can understand and remember it.

**Writer/Recorder**: Carefully records the best answers of the group on the worksheet or paper, edits what the group has written, gets the group members to check and sign the paper, then turns it in to the teacher.

**Materials Handler**: Gets any materials or equipment needed by the group, keeps track of them, and puts them carefully away.

**Encourager**: Watches to make certain that everyone is participating, and invites reluctant or silent members to contribute. Sample statements: "Jane, what do you think?" "Robert, do you have anything to add?" "Nancy, help us out." "Juanita, what are your ideas on this?"

**Checker**: Checks on the comprehension or learning of group members by asking them to explain or summarize material learned or discussed. Sample statements: "Terry, why did we decide on this answer for number two?" "James, explain how we got this answer." "Anne, summarize for us what we've decided here."

**Praiser**: Helps members feel good about their contributions to the group by telling them how helpful they are. This is a good role to assign to help combat "put-downs." Sample statements: "That's a good idea, Al." "Sharon, you're very helpful." "Karen, I like the way you've helped us." "Good job, John."

**Prober**: In a pleasant way, keeps the group from superficial answering by not allowing the members to agree too quickly. Agrees when satisfied that the group has explored all the possibilities. Sample statements: "What other possibilities are there for this problem or question?" "What else could we put here?" "Let's double-check this answer."

Some other role possibilities include: **Noise Monitor** (uses a non-verbal signal to remind group members to quiet down), **Energizer** (energizes the group when it starts lagging), **Summarizer** (summarizes the material so that group members can check it again), **Observer** (keeps track of how well the team members are collaborating), **Time Keeper**, and **Paraphraser**. Come up with roles that fit the task and your students.

## Identity Interdependence

**Positive identity interdependence** exists when the group establishes a mutual identity through a name, flag, motto, or song. English teachers may wish to give poet's names to groups (The Whitman's, Frost's, Cummings', and Hughes'). Science teachers can give famous scientists' names to groups. Teachers may let students think of their own group names, make a flag for their group, establish a group motto, or create some other symbol of their joint identity.

## Environmental Interdependence

**Environmental interdependence** exists when group members are bound together by the physical environment in some way. Examples include giving each group a specific area to meet in, putting chairs or desks together, having group members hold hands or put their arms around each other, requiring group members to have their feet touching in a circle as they work, or placing a rope fence around the group. A first grade teacher we once worked with made circles on the floor with masking tape and required all group members to be within the circle while they worked together. Being stranded in the barn's haymow with your older brother because he carelessly knocked over the ladder is another example of environmental interdependence.

## Conclusion

> *"Pull together. In the mountains you must depend on each other for survival."*

Willi Unsoeld

Within Yosemite National Park lies the famous Half Dome Mountain. The Half Dome is famous for its 2000 feet of soaring, sheer cliff wall. Unusually beautiful to the observer, and considered unclimbable for years, the Half Dome's northwest face was first scaled in 1957 by Royal Robbins and two companions. This incredibly dangerous climb took five days, with Robbins and his companions spending four nights on the cliff, sleeping in ropes with nothing below their bodies but air. Even today, the northwest face is a death trap to all but the finest and most skilled rock climbers. And far above the ground, moving slowly up the rock face, are two climbers.

The two climbers are motivated by a shared vision of successfully climbing the northwest face. As they move up the cliff they are attached to each other by a rope (**"the life line"**). As one member climbs (**the lead climber**), the other (**the belayer**) ensures that the two have a safe anchor and that he or she can catch the climber if the climber falls. The lead climber does not begin climbing until the belayer says "go." Then the lead climber advances, puts in a piton, slips in the rope, and continues to advance. The pitons help the belayer catch the climber if the climber falls and they mark the path up the cliff. The life line (i.e., rope) goes from the belayer through the pitons up to the climber. When the lead climber has completed the first leg of the climb, he or she becomes the belayer and the other member of the team begins to climb. The pitons placed by the lead climber serve to guide and support the second member of the team up the rock face.

The second member advances up the route marked out by the first member until the first leg is completed, and then leap-frogs and becomes the lead climber for the second leg of the climb. The roles of lead climber and belayer are alternated until the summit is reached.

All human life is like mountain climbing. The human species seems to have a **cooperation imperative**: We desire and seek out opportunities to operate jointly with others to achieve mutual goals. We are attached to others through a variety of "life lines" and we alternate supporting and leading others to ensure a better life for ourselves, our colleagues and neighbors, our children, and all generations to follow. Cooperation is an inescapable fact of life. From cradle to grave we cooperate with others. Each day, from our first waking moment until sleep overtakes us again, we cooperate within family, work, leisure, and community by working jointly to achieve mutual goals. Throughout history, people have come together to (1) accomplish feats that any one of them could not achieve alone and (2) share their joys and sorrows. From conceiving a child to sending a rocket to the moon, our successes require cooperation among individuals. The cooperation may be less clear than it is in climbing up a cliff, but it exists none the less.

Cooperative efforts begin when group members commit themselves to a mutual purpose and coordinate and integrate their efforts to do so. What is true of the real life needs to be true of classroom life. In the classroom, the mutual purpose and coordinated actions spring from the positive interdependence structured by you, the teacher. By structuring positive interdependence you remind your students, **None of us is as smart as all of us!**

The more ways you structure positive interdependence within learning groups, the better. **Never use one when two will do.** Many students are highly competitive and will initially not believe that they really do have to help others learn. Given that every cooperative lesson must include mutual goals, the more ways positive interdependence is structured within a lesson, the clearer the message will be to students that they must be concerned about and take responsibility for both their own and other's learning. The real test of whether or not positive inter-dependence has been successfully structured is whether group members really care about each other's learning. If they do not care whether or not groupmates learn, then they do not really believe that they sink or swim together.

# Reducing Problem Behaviors

When students first start working in cooperative learning groups they sometimes engage in unhelpful behaviors. Whenever inappropriate student behavior occurs, the teacher's first move should be toward strengthening the perceived interdependence within the learning situation. When you see students not participating or not bringing their work or materials, you may wish to increase positive interdependence by jigsawing materials, assigning the student a role that is essential to the group's success, or rewarding the group on the basis of their average performance (thus increasing the peer pressure on the student to participate).

When a student is talking about everything **but** the assignment, you may wish to give a reward that this student or group finds especially attractive and structure the task so that all members must work steadily and contribute in order for the group to succeed and attain the reward.

When you see a student working alone and ignoring the group discussion, you may wish to limit the resources in the group (if there is only one answer sheet or pencil in the group, the member will be unable to work independently) or jigsaw materials so that the student cannot do the work without the other members' information.

When you see a student refusing to let other members participate or bullying other members you may wish to jigsaw resources, assign roles so that other group members have the most powerful roles, or reward the group on the basis of the lowest two scores by group members on a unit test.

# Positive Interdependence And Giving Grades

Ideally, each student in your classes will participate in a variety of cooperative, competitive, and individualistic instructional activities over the grading period. When summative grades are to be given, the number of points each student received in all three types of goal structures are added up to summarize achievement. A criterion-referenced evaluation procedure will have to be used if the student is to receive a specific single grade; a norm-referenced evaluation procedure will undermine all cooperative and individualistic learning activities in the future.

Grades represent the most common reward given in most classrooms. Current grading systems, however, have created a tragedy within many schools in America. Almost every child comes to school optimistic about his or her chances for success. Most end up believing they are failures and losers. Ask first-grade students entering school how they are going to do academically. Most will respond, "I am going to do well." By the end of second grade, however, many are not so sure. By the end of elementary school, many students believe they are not intelligent and are poor students.

One cause of this tragedy is the evaluation and recognition systems used in our classrooms. Some students consistently receive recognition and other students receive little or no recognition. There are winners and there are losers.

The situation is changed dramatically when high-, medium-, and low-achieving students are placed in a cooperative learning group. When the group succeeds, all members are recognized as having contributed to their joint success. Even low-ability students believe, **we** can succeed, **we** are successful. Being part of a cooperative learning group empowers each student by increasing his or her self-efficacy--the belief that if effort is exerted, success is possible. All students are recognized as contributing to the group's success. How to give grades to communicate to students that they "sink or swim together" is one of the most difficult aspects of structuring learning situations cooperatively. Here are a number of suggestions.

1. **Individual score plus bonus points based on all members reaching criterion**: Group members study together and ensure that all have mastered the assigned material. Each then takes a test individually and is awarded that score. If all group members achieve over a preset criterion of excellence, each receives a bonus. An example is as follows:

| Criteria for Bonus Points | | Group | Scores | Total |
|---|---|---|---|---|
| 100 | 15 points | Bill | 100 | 110 |
| 90 - 99 | 10 points | Sally | 90 | 100 |
| 80 - 89 | 5 points | Jane | 95 | 105 |

2. **Individual score plus bonus points based on lowest score**: The group members prepare each other to take an exam. Members then receive bonus points on the basis of the lowest individual score in their group. An example is as follows:

| Criteria for Bonus Points | | Group | Scores | Total |
|---|---|---|---|---|
| 71 - 75 | 1 point | Bill | 100 | 103 |
| 76 - 80 | 2 points | Sally | 98 | 101 |
| 81 - 85 | 3 points | Jane | 84 | 87 |
| 86 - 90 | 4 points | | | |
| 91 - 95 | 5 points | | | |
| 96 - 100 | 6 points | | | |

This procedure emphasizes encouraging, supporting, and assisting the low achievers in the group. The criterion for bonus points can be adjusted for each learning group, depending on the past performance of their lowest member.

3. **Individual score plus bonus based on improvement scores**: Members of a cooperative group prepare each other to take an exam. Each takes the exam individually and receives his or her individual grade. In addition, bonus points are awarded on the basis of whether members percentage on

the current test is higher than the average percentage on all past tests (i.e., their usual level of performance). Their percentage correct on past tests serves as their base score that they try to better. Every two tests or scores, the base score is updated. If a student scores within 4 points (above or below) his or her base score, all members of the group receive 1 bonus point. If they score 5 to 9 points above their base score, each group member receives 2 bonus points. Finally, if they score 10 points or above their base score, or score 100 percent correct, each member receives 3 bonus points.

4. **Group score on a single product**: The group works to produce a single report, essay, presentation, worksheet, or exam. The product is evaluated and all members receive the score awarded. When this method is used with worksheets, sets of problems, and examinations, group members are required to reach consensus on each question and be able to explain it to others. The discussion within the group enhances the learning considerably.

5. **Randomly selecting one member's paper to score**: Group members all complete the work individually and then check each other's papers and certify that they are perfectly correct. Since each paper is certified by the whole group to be correct, it makes little difference which paper is graded. The teacher picks one at random, grades it, and all group members receive the score.

6. **Average of academic scores plus collaborative skills performance score**: Group members work together to master the assigned material. They take an examination individually and their scores are averaged. Concurrently, their work is observed and the frequency of performance of specified collaborative skills (such as leadership or trust-building actions) is recorded. The group is given a collaborative skills performance score, which is added to their academic average to determine their overall mark.

# Conclusions

In revisiting Sugar Loaf Hill in Okinawa William Manchester gained an important insight. "I understand at last, why I jumped hospital that long-ago Sunday and, in violation of orders, returned to the front and almost certain death. It was an act of love. Those men on the line were my family, my home. They were closer to me than I can say, closer than any friends had been or ever would be. They were comrades; three of them had saved my life. They had never let me down, and I couldn't do it to them. I had to be with them, rather than let them die and me live with the knowledge that I might have saved them. Men, I now knew, do not fight for flag or country, for the Marine Corps or glory or any other abstraction. They fight for their friends."

Positive interdependence results in individuals striving together to achieve mutual goals which, in turn, promotes caring and committed relationships. The more caring and committed the relationships, furthermore, the more interdependent individuals will perceive themselves to be and the more individuals will dedicate themselves to achieving the group's goals. Positive interdependence is the essence of cooperative learning. There are a number of ways of structuring positive interdependence. Teachers may structure positive goal interdependence, reward interdependence, resource interdependence, role interdependence, task interdependence, outside enemy interdependence, fantasy interdependence, identity interdependence, and environmental interdependence. The more types of positive interdependence teachers structure, the more effective cooperative learning will be. Many of the problems in student participation within learning groups may be prevented or resolved through the systematic use of positive interdependence. Grades are one of the ways in which students are given the message, "We sink or swim together."

After positive interdependence is carefully structured, teachers may wish to focus on teaching students the cooperative skills they need to function effectively within the learning groups. The next chapter focuses on this topic.

# Chapter 5

# Teaching Students Cooperative Skills

## The Importance of Cooperative Skills

> "...instead of looking on discussion as a stumbling-block in the way of action, we think it an indispensable preliminary to any wise action at all."

Pericles

Children are not born instinctively knowing how to interact effectively with others. Interpersonal and group skills do not magically appear when they are needed. Students must be taught these skills and be motivated to use them. Many elementary and secondary students lack basic social skills such as correctly identifying the emotions of others and appropriately discussing an assignment. Their social ineptitude seems to persist into adulthood. Students who lack appropriate social skills find themselves isolated, alienated, and at a disadvantage in career training programs. It has often been estimated that over 10 percent of school children have no friends and perhaps a third of school children are not especially liked by any of their peers. Poor peer relationships have widespread immediate and long-term effects on children's cognitive and social development, well-being, happiness, success, and psychological health.

There is no way to overemphasize the importance of the skills required to work effectively with others. **Cooperative skills are the keystones to maintaining a stable family, a successful career, and a stable group of friends.** These skills have to be taught just as purposefully and precisely as reading and math skills. While many social skills are usually learned in family and community experiences, many contemporary children and adolescents lack basic social skills. One of the great advantages of cooperative learning is that important "life-survival" skills are required, used, reinforced, and mastered within a task situation. Participating in cooperative learning situations requires students to develop and use the social skills necessary for living productive and fulfilling lives as adults.

Since many students have never been taught how to work effectively with others, they cannot do so. Thus, the first experience of many teachers who try structuring lessons cooperatively is that their students cannot collaborate with each other. Teaching cooperative skills becomes an important prerequisite for academic learning since achievement will improve as students become more effective in learning from each other. It is within cooperative situations, where there is a task to complete, that social skills become most relevant and should ideally be taught. All students need to become skillful in communicating, building and maintaining trust, providing leadership, engaging in fruitful controversy, and managing conflicts (Johnson, 1987, 1990; Johnson & F. Johnson, 1987).

In this chapter we will review some of the assumptions that are vital to teaching cooperative skills, list and discuss some of the social skills, and describe a model for teaching them.

## Teaching Cooperative Skills: Assumptions

There are four assumptions underlying teaching students cooperative skills. **The first is that prior to teaching the skills a cooperative context must be established.** The intent of cooperative learning is to create a perception that students "sink or swim together" and, therefore, must be actively involved in maximizing their own learning while at the same time maximizing the learning of groupmates. It is not to "win." When these overall cooperative goals are lacking, interaction among students becomes competitive, hostile, divisive, and destructive. Students who are competing want to "win," not learn the skills to cooperate. It makes little sense, furthermore, to teach students how to work more effectively with each other if they are expected to spend the school day working alone without interacting with classmates. Students' awareness of the need for collaborative skills is directly related to their being in cooperative situations. Implementing cooperative learning is vital to increasing students' collaborative competencies.

**Second, cooperative skills have to be directly taught.** Structuring lessons cooperatively is not enough. Students are not born with the interpersonal and group skills required to collaborate with each other, nor do the skills magically appear when the students need them. Learning how to interact effectively with others is no different from learning how to use a microscope, play a piano, write a complete sentence, or read. The same basic process is required for all skill learning.

**Third, while it is the teacher who structures cooperation within the classroom and initially defines the skills required to collaborate, it is the other group members who largely determine whether the skills are learned and internalized.** Teachers rely on the student's peers to cue and monitor the use of the skills, give feedback on how well the skills are being enacted, and reinforce their appropriate use. Peer accountability to learn cooperative skills must always be coupled with peer support for doing so. Group members need to communicate both, "We want you to practice this collaborative skill," and "How can we help you do so?" After the teacher instructs students as to what the cooperative skills are, and encourages students to practice the skills in their learning groups, peer support and feedback will determine whether the skills are used appropriately and frequently enough for the skills to be natural and automatic actions. Peer feedback will occur subtly while the groups are working and directly in formal feedback sessions structured by the teacher.

**Fourth, the earlier students are taught cooperative skills, the better.** There are procedures for kindergarten and even preschool teachers to use in teaching students collaborative skills. In elementary, secondary, and post-secondary settings teachers should be involved in improving students' competencies in work-

# Constructing A T-Chart

1. Write the name of the skill to be learned and practiced and draw a large T underneath..

2. Title the left side of the T "Looks Like" and the right side of the T "Sounds Like."

3. On the left side write a number of behaviors that operationalize the skill. On the right side write a number of phrases that operationalize the skill.

4. Have all students practice "Looks Like" and "Sounds Like" several times before the lesson is conducted.

## Encouraging Participation

| Looks Like | Sounds Like |
|---|---|
| Thumbs Up | "What is your idea?" |
| Smiles | "Good idea!" |
| Eye Contact | "Awesome!" |
| Pat On the Back | That's interesting." |

ing collaboratively with each other. To inform adults who are engineers, managers, supervisors, or secretaries that they need to learn how to cooperate more effectively with others is important, but a little late. Their education should have prepared them for the cooperation inherent in adult career and family life. There is a direct relation between schools demanding that students work alone without interacting with each other and the number of adults in our society who lack the competencies required to work effectively with others in career, family, and leisure settings.

# What Skills Need To Be Taught?

John Dugan, in his 11th-grade English class in Suffern, New York, begins a unit on grammar with teaching students a set of leadership skills. He structures **positive interdependence** by giving students the assignment of (1) mastering the leadership skills and (2) ensuring that all members of their group master the leadership skills. The leadership skills he teaches are:

1. **Direction Giver**: Gives direction to the group's work by:

    a. Reviewing the instructions and restating the purpose of the assignment.

    b. Calling attention to the time limits.

    c. Offering procedures on how to complete the assignment most effectively.

2. **Summarizer**: Summarizes out loud what has just been read or discussed as completely as possible without referring to notes or to the original material.

3. **Generator**: Generates additional answers by going beyond the first answer or conclusion and producing a number of plausible answers to choose from.

The process he uses to teach the skills is as follows. **First**, he explains the skills. **Second**, he models the skills by demonstrating them. **Third**, he asks the class to generate a series of phrases that could be used to engage in the skills, such as "One way we could do this is...," "Another answer is..." **Fourth**, he next selects three students to role play a group session in front of the class in which the leadership skills are used. After the role play the whole class discusses each of the skills again. **Fifth**, students are told to complete the first grammar assignment while using the three leadership skills as frequently as possible. **Individual accountability** is structured by observing each group to verify that each group member engages in at least two of the three targeted leadership skills. John circulates throughout the room, systematically observing each group, recording how frequently each leadership role is engaged in. Groups in which each member engages in at least two of the leadership behaviors receive five bonus points on the first grammar assignment (**positive reward interdependence**).

There are numerous interpersonal skills that affect the success of collaborative efforts (Johnson, 1990, 1987; Johnson & F. Johnson, 1987; Johnson & R. Johnson, 1987). What cooperative skills teachers emphasize in their classes depends on what their students have and have not mastered. As teachers observe and monitor their students working in cooperative learning groups the teachers will notice where students lack important skills. Our list of required student behaviors may give teachers a starting point in examining how skillful their students are. There are four levels of cooperative skills:

1. **Forming**: The bottom-line skills needed to establish a functioning cooperative learning group.

2. **Functioning**: The skills needed to manage the group's activities in completing the task and in maintaining effective working relationships among members.

3. **Formulating**: The skills needed to build deeper-level understanding of the material being studied, to stimulate the use of higher quality reasoning strategies, and to maximize mastery and retention of the assigned material.

4. **Fermenting**: The skills needed to stimulate reconceptualization of the material being studied, cognitive conflict, the search for more information, and the communication of the rationale behind one's conclusions.

## Forming

**Forming skills** are an initial set of management skills directed toward organizing the group and establishing minimum norms for appropriate behavior. Some of the more important behaviors in this category are:

1. **Moving into cooperative learning groups without undue noise and without bothering others**: Work time in groups is a valuable commodity and little time should be spent in rearranging furniture and moving into learning groups. Students may need to practice the procedure for getting into groups several times before they become efficient in doing so.

2. **Staying with the group**: Moving around the room during group time is nonproductive for the student doing it as well as for the other group members.

3. **Using quiet voices**: Cooperative learning groups do not need to be noisy and can learn to work very quietly. Some teachers assign one student in each group to make sure that everyone speaks softly.

4. **Encouraging everyone to participate**: All group members need to share their ideas and materials and be part of the group's efforts to achieve. Taking turns is one way to formalize this.

5. **Other forming skills** include:

   a. Keeping your hands (and feet) to yourself.

   b. Looking at the paper.

   c. Using names.

   d. Looking at the speaker.

   e. Eliminating "put-downs."

## Functioning

The second level of cooperative skills are the **functioning skills** involved in managing the group's efforts to complete their tasks and maintain effective working relationships among members. Some of these skills are:

1. **Giving direction** to the group's work by:

   a. Stating and restating the purpose of the assignment.

   b. Setting or calling attention to time limits.

   c. Offering procedures on how to most effectively complete the assignment.

2. **Expressing support and acceptance** both verbally and nonverbally through eye contact, interest, praising, and seeking others' ideas and conclusions.

3. **Asking for help or clarification** of what is being said or done in the group.

4. **Offering to explain or clarify**.

5. **Paraphrasing** and clarifying another member's contributions.

6. **Energizing** the group when motivation is low by suggesting new ideas, through humor, or by being enthusiastic.

7. **Describing one's feelings** when appropriate.

The mixture of keeping members on task, finding effective and efficient work procedures, and fostering a pleasant and friendly work atmosphere is vital for effective leadership in cooperative learning groups.

## Formulating

**Formulating skills** are needed to provide the mental processes needed to build deeper level understanding of the material being studied, to stimulate the use of higher quality reasoning strategies, and to maximize mastery and retention of the assigned material. Since the purpose of learning groups is to maximize the learning of all members, there are skills specifically aimed at providing formal methods for processing the material being studied. They include:

1. **Summarizer**: Summarizing out loud what has just been read or discussed as completely as possible without referring to notes or to the original material. All the important ideas and facts should be included in the summary. Every member of the group must summarize from memory often if their learning is to be maximized.

2. **Corrector**: Seeking accuracy by correcting a member's summary, adding important information he or she did not include, and pointing out the ideas or facts that were summarized incorrectly.

3. **Elaboration Seeker**: Seeking elaboration by asking other members to relate the material being learned to earlier material and to other things they know.

4. **Memory Helper**: Seeking clever ways of remembering the important ideas and facts by using drawings, mental pictures, and other memory aids.

5. **Checker**: Demanding vocalization to make the implicit reasoning process being used by other members overt and thus open to correction and discussion.

6. **Explanation Checker**: Asking other members to plan out loud how they would teach another student the material being studied. Planning how best to communicate the material can have important effects on quality of reasoning strategies and retention.

## Fermenting

**Fermenting** includes the skills needed to engage in **academic controversies** to stimulate reconceptualization of the material being studied, cognitive conflict, the search for more information, and the communication of the rationale behind one's conclusions. Some of the most important aspects of learning take place when group members skillfully challenge each other's conclusions and reasoning (Johnson & R. Johnson, 1987, 1989). Academic controversies cause group members to "dig deeper" into the material, to assemble a rationale for their conclusions, to think more divergently about the issue, to find more information to support their positions, and to argue constructively about alternative solutions or decisions. Some of the skills involved in academic controversies are:

1. Criticizing ideas without criticizing people.

2. Differentiating where there is disagreement within the learning group.

3. Integrating a number of different ideas into a single position.

4. Asking for justification why the member's conclusion or answer is the correct or appropriate one.

5. Extending another member's answer or conclusion by adding further information or implications.

6. Probing by asking questions that lead to deeper understanding or analysis ("Would it work in this situation . . .?" "What else makes you believe . . .?").

7. Generating further answers by going beyond the first answer or conclusion and producing a number of plausible answers to choose from.

8. Testing reality by checking out the group's work with the instructions, available time, and other examples of reality.

These skills are among those that keep group members motivated to go beyond the quick answer to the highest quality one. They are aimed at stimulating the thinking and intellectual curiosity of group members.

## Summary

Typically, teachers begin with the forming skills to ensure that the group members are present and oriented toward working with each other. The functioning skills then assist the group in operating smoothly and building constructive relationships among members. The formulating skills ensure that high quality learning takes place within the group and that the members engage in the necessary cognitive processing. The fermenting skills are the most complex and the most difficult to master. They ensure that intellectual challenge and disagreement take place within the learning groups.

The above skills are discussed in terms of upper elementary, secondary, and post-secondary students. Primary and preschool students will need simplified versions of the skills. It is important that teachers translate cooperative skills into language and images that their students can understand and identify with. For example, the fermenting skills could be simplified to skills such as adding an idea, asking for proof, and seeing the idea from the other person's shoes.

# How Do You Teach Cooperative Skills?

Learning cooperative skills is first of all procedural learning, very similar to learning how to play tennis or golf, how to perform brain surgery, or how to fly an airplane. Being skilled in managing conflicts involves more than simply reading material for a recognition-level or even a total-recall-level of mastery. It requires learning a procedure that is made up of a series of actions. **Procedural learning** exists when individuals:

1. Learn conceptually what the skill is and when it should be appropriately used.

2. Translate their conceptual understanding into a set of operational procedures (phrases and actions) appropriate for the people they are interacting with.

3. Actually engage in the skill.

4. Eliminate errors by moving through the phases of skill mastery.

5. Attain a routine-use, automated level of mastery.

Procedural learning involves breaking a complex process into its component parts and then systematically learning the process until it becomes automatic. It differs from simply learning facts and acquiring knowledge by relying heavily on feedback about performance and modifying one's implementation until the errors of performance are eliminated. It is a gradual process--one's efforts to perform the skill will fail to match the ideal of what one wishes to accomplish for a considerable length of time until the new strategy is overlearned at a routine-use, automated level. Failure is part of the process of gaining expertise, and success is inevitable when failure is followed by persistent practice, obtaining feedback, and reflecting on how to perform the skill more competently. Any complex process is best learned if it is proceduralized. The ultimate goal of procedural learning is to have students automatically perform the skill without having to think about it.

Learning a cooperative skill results from a process of:

1. Engaging in the skill.

2. Obtaining feedback.

3. Reflecting on the feedback.

4. Modifying one's enactment and engaging in the skill again.

5. Repeating steps 2, 3, and 4 again and again and again until the skill is appropriately used in a more and more automated fashion.

Gaining expertise takes "learning partners" who are willing to trust each other, talk frankly, and observe each other's performance over a prolonged period of time and help each other identify the errors being made in implementing the skill. Unless students are willing to reveal lack of expertise to obtain accurate feedback, expertise cannot be gained. In other words, procedural learning, and the mastery of all skills, requires cooperation among students.

One of the most important aspects of conducting cooperative learning lessons is identifying the students who are having difficulty in arguing effectively because of missing or underdeveloped cooperative skills. The part of the teacher's role dealing with monitoring highlights the importance of gathering data on students as they work and intervening to encourage more appropriate behavior. Teachers often assume that students have the social skills necessary for working cooperatively with others. This is often not the case, even when students are in high school or college. Family background, role models and the nature of the students' peer group all influence the development of such skills. The exciting part of teaching students to be more effective working with others is that the students not only gain a valuable set of skills for life, but have an excellent chance of raising their achievement as well.

There are five major steps in teaching cooperative skills:

1. Ensuring students **see the need** for the skill.

2. Ensuring students **understand** what the skill is and when it should be used.

3. Setting up **practice** situations and encouraging mastery of the skill.

4. Ensuring that students have the time and the needed **procedures for processing** (and receiving feedback on) how well they are using the skill.

5. Ensuring that students **persevere** in practicing the skill until the skill seems a natural action.

## Step 1: Helping Students See the Need for the Skill

To be motivated to learn cooperative skills, students must believe that they are better off knowing, than not knowing, the skills. Teachers can promote students' awareness of the need for cooperative skills by:

1. **Displaying** in the room posters, bulletin boards, and other evidence that the teacher considers the skills to be important. It is often easy to see what is important in a classroom by looking at the walls, boards, and seating arrangements of the room.

2. **Communicating** to students why mastering the skills is important. With many students, sharing information about the need for cooperative skills in career and family settings is enough. Other students may benefit from experiencing how the skills help them do better work.

3. **Validating** the importance of the skills by assigning a grade or giving a reward to groups whose members demonstrate competence in the skills. Many teachers give learning groups two grades: one for achievement and one for the appropriate use of targeted cooperative skills.

There are other ways to communicate the importance of cooperative skills--covering the walls with postures, telling students how important the skills are, and rewarding students who use the skill, get teachers off to a good start.

## Step 2: Ensuring Students Understand What the Skill Is

To learn a skill, students must have a clear idea of what the skill is and how to perform it. There is little chance of being too concrete in defining cooperative skills. Every student needs to know what to say or do to perform the skill. A number of strategies teachers can use in ensuring students understand what a skill is and when it is to be appropriately used are:

1. **Helping students generate specific phrases and be-haviors that express the skill.** "Do you agree?" asks for a "yes" or "no" answer and is, therefore, a much less effec-tive encouraging question than is "How would you explain the answer?" The class may wish to list phrases the teacher should hear in each group as the teacher monitors the group's effectiveness. The list can then be prominently displayed for reference.

2. **Demonstrating, modeling, and having students role play the skill** are all effective procedures for clearly defin-ing the skill. Setting up a short counter-example where the skill is obviously missing is one way to emphasize the skill and illustrate the need for it at the same time.

Teachers should not try to teach too many skills at the same time. Start with one or two. One first-grade curriculum unit we have helped with teaches eight skills over a year's time, starting with "Everyone does a job" and including "Sharing ideas and materials," "Giving directions without being bossy," and "Caring about others' feelings."

## Step 3: Setting Up Repetitive Practice Situations

**To master a skill, students need to practice it again and again.** Students should be asked to role play the skill several times with the person sitting next to them immediately after the skill is defined. An initial practice session should be long enough for the skill to be fairly well learned by each student, and then short practice sessions should be distributed across several days or weeks. As students practice, teachers should continue to give verbal instructions and encourage students to perform the skills with proper sequence and timing. Some of the strategies found effective for encouraging practice are:

1. **Assigning specific roles to group members to ensure practice of the skills.** A teacher, for example, could as-sign the roles of reader, encourager, summarizer, and elaboration-seeker to the members of a cooperative learn-

ing group. The roles could be rotated daily until every student has been responsible for each role several times.

2. **Announcing that the occurrence of the skills will be observed.** It is surprising how much practice of a skill occurs when the teacher announces that he or she will be looking for a specific skill and stands next to a group with an observation sheet. The teacher's presence and the knowledge that the frequency of the skills is being counted and valued by the teacher (or a student observer) is a potent motivater of practice.

3. **Using nonacademic skill-building exercises to provide students with a chance to practice cooperative skills.** There may be times when an exercise that is fun and not part of the ongoing work of the class can be used to encourage students to practice specific skills. There are many such exercises available (Johnson, 1987, 1990; Johnson & F. Johnson, 1987; Johnson & R. Johnson, 1987).

New skills need to be cued consistently and reinforced for some time. Teachers should be relentless in encouraging prolonged use of cooperative skills.

## Step 4: Ensuring That Students Process Their Use of the Skills

Practicing cooperative skills is not enough. **Students must process how frequently and how well they are using the skill.** Students need to discuss, describe, and reflect on their use of the skills in order to improve their performance. To ensure that students discuss and give each other feedback about their use of the skills, teachers need to provide a regular time for group processing and give students group processing procedures to follow. The following strategies may help:

1. **Provide regular time for processing.** Ten minutes at the end of each period, or 20 minutes once a week are typical.

2. **Provide a set of procedures for students to follow.** A processing sheet that the group fills out together, signs, and then hands in may be useful. Questions might include, "How many members felt they had a chance to share their ideas in their group?" and "How many members felt listened to?" The most effective procedure, however, is to have one member of the group observe the frequency with which each member engages in one of the targeted conflict management skills and, in the discussion at the end of the period, give each member feedback about his or her performance.

3. **Provide opportunities for positive feedback among group members.** One procedure is to have each member told by every other member one action that reflected effective use of a conflict management skill.

A standard processing task is, "Name three things your group did well and name one thing your group could do even better next time." Such group processing will not only increase students' interpersonal and small group skills, it will also increase achievement (Johnson, Johnson, Stanne, & Garibaldi, in press; Yager, Johnson, & Johnson, 1985) and the quality of the relationships developed among students (Putnan, Johnson, Rynders, & Johnson, 1989). Teachers may have to model the processing initially and periodically so that students will take the processing seriously and become adept at doing it.

## Step 5: Ensuring That Students Persevere in Practicing the Skills

With most skills there is a period of slow learning, then a period of rapid improvement, then a period where performance remains about the same, then another period of rapid improvement, then another plateau, and so forth. **Students have to practice cooperative skills long enough to make it through the first few plateaus and integrate the skills into their behavioral repertoires.** There are a set of stages that most skill development goes through:

1. **Awareness** that the skill is needed.

2. **Understanding** of what the skill is.

3. Self-conscious, **awkward engaging** in the skill. Practicing any new skill feels awkward. The first few times someone throws a football, plays a piano, or paraphrases, it feels strange.

4. Feelings of **phoniness** while **engaging** in the skill. After a while the awkwardness passes and enacting the skill becomes more smooth. Many students, however, feel unauthentic or phony while using the skill. Teacher and peer encouragement are needed to move the students through this stage.

5. Skilled but **mechanical use** of the skill.

6. **Automatic, routine use** where the skill is fully integrated into students' behavior repertoire and seems like a natural action to engage in.

Ways to ensure that students persevere are to continue to assign the skill as a group role, continue to give students feedback as to how frequently and how well they are performing the skill, and reinforcing the groups when members use the skill.

## Using Bonus Points To Teach Social Skills

Many teachers may want to use a structured program to teach students the interpersonal and small group skills they need to cooperative effectively with classmates. Such a program will provide students with the opportunity to help earn bonus points for their groups as a result of their using targeted cooperative skills. These points can be accumulated for academic credit or for special rewards such as free time or minutes listening to one's own choice of music. The procedure for doing so is as follows:

1. Identify, define, and teach a social skill you want students to use in working cooperatively with each other. This skill becomes a target for mastery. The skills may be **forming** skills of staying with your group and using quiet voices, **functioning** skills of giving direction to the group's work and encouraging participation, **formulating** skills of explaining answers, relating present learning to past learning, and **fermenting** skills of criticizing ideas without criticizing people, asking probing questions, and requesting further rationale (Johnson, Johnson, & Holubec, 1988).

2. Use group points and group rewards to increase the use of the cooperative skill:

   a. Each time a student engages in the targeted skill, the student's group receives a point.

   b. Points may only be awarded for positive behavior.

   c. Points are added and never taken away. All points are permanently earned.

3. Summarize total points daily. Emphasize daily progress toward the goal. Use a visual display such as a graph or chart.

4. Develop an observational system that samples each group an equal amount of time. In addition, utilize student observers to record the frequency of students using the targeted skills.

5. Set a reasonable number of points for earning the reward. Rewards are both social and tangible. The social reward is having the teacher say, "That shows thought," "I like the way you explained it," "That's a good way of putting it," "Remarkably well done." The tangible reward is the points earned, which may be traded in for free time, computer time, library time, time to a play a game, extra recess time, and any other activity that students value.

6. In addition to group points, class points may be awarded. The teacher, for example, might say, "Eighteen people are ready to begin and helped the class earn a reward," or "I noticed 12 people worked the last 25 minutes." Class points may be recorded with a number line, beans in a jar, or checks on the chalk board.

7. In addition to social skills, potential target behaviors include following directions, completing assigned tasks, handing in homework, behaving appropriately in out-of-class settings such as lunch or assemblies, or helping substitute teachers.

# Conclusion

If the potential of cooperative learning is to be realized, students must have the prerequisite interpersonal and small group skills and be motivated to use them. These skills need to be taught just as systematically as math and social studies. Doing so involves communicating to students the need for the social skills, defining and modeling the skills, having students practice the skills over and over again, processing how effectively the students are performing the skills, and ensuring that students persevere until the skills are fully integrated into their behavioral repertoires. Doing so will not only increase student achievement, it will also increase students' future employability, career success, quality of relationships, and psychological health.

Nothing we learn is more important than the skills required to work cooperatively with other people. Most human interaction is cooperative. Without some skill in cooperating effectively, it is difficult (if not impossible) to maintain a marriage, hold a job, or be part of a community, society, and world. In this chapter we have only discussed a few of the interpersonal and small group skills needed for effective cooperation. For a more thorough and extensive coverage of these skills see **Reaching Out** (Johnson, 1990), **Joining Together** (Johnson & F. Johnson, 1987), **Human Relations and Your Career** (Johnson, 1987), and **Learning Together And Alone** (Johnson & R. Johnson, 1987).

# Chapter 6

# Cooperation Among Teachers

## Implementing Cooperative Learning

### Introduction

Cooperation among students will be easier to establish and maintain if there is cooperation among school personnel. Many
schools are scarred by competition among teachers. In these
schools, teachers feel insecure, isolated, cold, reserved, defensive, and competitive in their relationships with fellow teachers
and administrators. Feelings of hostility, guardedness, and aliena-
tion toward the rest of the school staff create anxiety in teachers,
which in turn decreases their effectiveness in the classroom. The
teachers act as though they never need help from their colleagues. A fiction is maintained that a "professional and highly
trained teacher" has already achieved sufficient competence and
skill to handle all classroom situations alone. The actual result,
however, is that innovative and creative teaching is stifled by in-
security, anxiety, and competitiveness. And the school environment is depressing and discouraging.

**One of the most constructive contributions you can make to
your school is to encourage cooperation among teachers
and the use of cooperative learning in the classroom.** How
do you encourage teacher cooperation? The process is the
same as for implementing cooperation among students. Establish cooperative goals that all involved teachers wish to accomplish and that require interdependence and interaction
among the teachers. Sufficient trust and openness must be
present for teachers to feel free to visit one another's classrooms

and ask one another for help or suggestions. Providing feedback about each other's teaching and providing help to increase teaching skills are equally important. Teachers must have the basic communication, trust building, decision-making, and controversy skills. Team teaching, coordinating all related curricula, establishing support groups in which teachers provide help and assistance to each other, coordinating the teaching of difficult students, are all examples of cooperative interaction among teachers.

## Developing Expertise In Cooperative Learning

Implementing new instructional practices in your classroom and your colleagial growth as a teacher require:

1. Taking risks by experimenting with new instructional strategies.

2. Accepting failure as:

    a. An inevitable result of experimentation.

    b. A source of learning about improving teaching practices.

3. Jointly reflecting with supportive colleagues about your implementation efforts.

Unfortunately, one of the major barriers to implementation is that teachers are expected never to fail and, if they do, they are expected to deny and hide it because it is viewed competitively as something shameful and as proof that they are incompetent (or less competent than other teachers). Teachers, in other words, are placed in a "bind" where they are supposed to be innovative but also supposed to magically master all new instructional strategies and implement them perfectly the first time they try.

Teachers do not become proficient in using cooperative learning procedures from attending a workshop or from reading this book. **Teachers become proficient and competent from**

**doing.** For teachers to develop the expertise in cooperative learning procedures they need to structure a cooperative lesson routinely without conscious planning or thought, they must:

1. Use cooperative learning procedures regularly for several years.

2. Jointly reflect on their experiences doing so with supportive and interested colleagues in ways that provide continuous and immediate:

   a. Feedback on quality of implementation.

   b. Assistance in developing lessons and materials.

   c. Help in solving problems and overcoming barriers.

**In order to perfect and expand the use of cooperative learning strategies teachers need a colleagial support group whose goal is to promote the continuous growth in competence in using cooperative learning.**

Both teachers and administrators may learn from their colleagues. In this chapter teachers are the primary referent for colleagial learning, but the statements made refer equally to colleagial learning among administrators. At times the chapter will refer to **cooperative learning leaders,** who are individuals within a school district involved in training teachers how to use cooperative learning procedures and strategies.

## Giving Up the Individualistic Perspective

**There is a myth in our society that the efficiency of work increases when individuals work alone, by themselves, without contact or interaction with others.** The more efficient way for work to be structured is assumed to be individualistic or competitive, where every person has his/her own space, materials, and goals, and works either to outperform his/her peers or to achieve up to a preset criteria of excellence. Other individuals are viewed as sources of disruption and distraction who lower performance and increase the amount of time necessary to complete the task. The purpose of one's work is to maximize one's own rewards.

Within many schools there is a diffuse and amorphous competition among teachers without clear rules, with no clear beginning or ending, and unclear criteria for determining winners and losers. In a recent study of teachers, for example, Ashton and Webb (1986) found that most teachers felt isolated from their colleagues, aware that their colleagues were highly judgmental, believed that the judgments were being made on fragmentary information, and believed that colleagues would not provide help and assistance to solve whatever problems the teachers were facing in their classrooms. Such conditions encouraged teachers to camouflage rather than confront their shortcomings and to exaggerate, to themselves and others, what they took to be their accomplishments. Most teachers worked to create the impression of competence by advertising their achievements, tempering their failures, and concealing their self-doubts. One teacher said that at her school it was well understood that you should "never let another teacher find a weakness or an area you need help in." She went on to say, "You can never go into a teachers' lounge and hear a teacher say, 'Damn, I really failed that kid today.' You never hear that. You always hear how a teacher was on top of a situation." A teacher stated that outright bragging about your competence was unwise. She stated, "Other teachers don't like that. Don't brag, because we are all competitors and we all think we're very intelligent."

No one should be surprised that when teachers spend their day teaching individualistic and competitive values to students, they themselves will come to believe in such values. Teachers who spend up to six hours a day telling students, "Do not copy," "I want to see what you can do, not your neighbor," "Let's see who is best," and "Who is the winner," will in turn tend to approach their colleagues with the attitudes of, "Don't copy from me," and "Who is the winner in implementing this new teaching strategy." **There is considerable evidence that people adopt the attitudes and values they espouse to others.** The result is that teachers view the school and their job from a competitive perspective and stop thinking of mutual benefit and think only of their own personal benefit, both of which are antithetical to organizational effectiveness.

**If teachers are to learn from each other, they must interact within a cooperative context.** A clear cooperative structure is the first prerequisite for effective colleagial learning. Like all cooperative groups, teacher colleagial support groups have to be structured to include positive interdependence, face-to-face promotive interaction, individual accountability for helping the group achieve its goals, and periodic group processing. In addition, the teachers must possess the required leadership, communication, trust-building, decision-making, and conflict-management skills.

# Colleagial Support Groups

For effective implementation of cooperative learning procedures within a school or a school district, concentrate your efforts on structuring and managing teacher colleagial support groups within each school building. A **colleagial support group** consists of three to five teachers who have the goal of improving each other's professional competence and ensuring each other's professional growth. **Colleagial support groups are first and foremost safe places where:**

1. Members like to be.

2. There is support, caring, concern, laughter, and camaraderie.

3. The primary goal of improving each other's competence in using cooperative learning procedures is never obscured.

Successfully implementing cooperative learning in the schools depends on creating such a support and assistance system among the teachers involved. **Teachers will not only teach each other how to use cooperative learning procedures but also sustain each other's interest in doing so.** Our best advice for long-term implementation of cooperative learning procedures is for you to form a professional support and assistance system among your interested colleagues.

**The purpose of this colleagial support group is to work jointly to improve continuously each other's competence in using cooperative learning procedures** or, in other words, to:

1. Help each other continue to gain competence in using cooperative learning procedures.

2. Serve as an informal support group for sharing, letting off steam, and discussing problems connected with implementing cooperative learning procedures.

3. Serve as a base for teachers experienced in the use of cooperative learning procedures to teach other teachers how to structure and manage lessons cooperatively.

4. Provide camaraderie and shared success.

**The three key activities of a collegial support group are** (Little, 1981):

1. Frequent professional discussions of cooperative learning in which information is shared, successes are celebrated, and problems connected with implementation are solved.

2. Coplanning, codesigning, copreparing, and coevaluating curriculum materials relevant to implementing cooperative learning in the classrooms of the members.

3. Coteaching and reciprocal observations of each other teaching lessons structured cooperatively and jointly processing those observations.

## Professional Discussions

Within the professional support groups there must be frequent, continuous, increasingly concrete and precise talk about the use of cooperative learning procedures. Through such discussion members build a concrete, precise, and coherent shared language that can describe the complexity of using cooperative learning procedures, distinguish one practice and its virtues from another, and integrate cooperative learning procedures into other teaching practices and strategies that they are already using. Through such discussions, teachers will exchange successful procedures and materials. They will focus on solving specific problems members may be having in perfecting their use of cooperative learning strategies.

## Joint Planning and Curriculum Design

Members of professional support groups should frequently plan, design, prepare, and evaluate curriculum materials together. This results in teachers sharing the burden of developing materials needed to conduct cooperative lessons, generating emerging understanding of cooperative learning strategies, making realistic standards for students and colleagues, and providing the machinery for each other to implement cooperative learning procedures. The process of planning a lesson together, each conducting it, and then processing it afterwards is often constructive.

## Reciprocal Observations

Members of professional support groups should frequently observe each other teaching lessons structured cooperatively and then provide each other with useful feedback. This observation and feedback provide members with shared experiences to discuss and refer to. Teachers especially need to treat each other with the deference that shows they recognize that anyone can have good and bad days and that the mistakes they note in a colleague may be the same mistakes that they will make tomorrow.

We have found a number of important guidelines that we have teachers follow when they are observing the teaching of other members of their colleagial support group. These **guidelines** include:

1. Realize that you can learn from every other member of the group, regardless of their experience and personal characteristics.

2. Make sure observation and feedback is reciprocal.

3. Ask the person you're observing what he/she would like you to focus your attention on. This may include specific students the teacher may wish observed, specific aspects of structuring interdependence or accountability, or some other aspect of cooperative learning.

4. Focus feedback and comments on what has taken place, not on personal competence.

5. Don't confuse a teacher's personal worth with her/his current level of competence in using cooperative learning procedures.

6. Be concrete and practical in your discussions about how effectively members are using cooperative learning procedures.

7. Above all, communicate respect for each other's overall teaching competence. We all have professional strengths and weaknesses. Recognize and respect those strengths in each other.

Working collaboratively with others brings with it camaraderie, friendship, warmth, satisfaction, and feelings of success. These are all to be enjoyed.

## Helpful Norms

There are a number of helpful norms for colleagial support groups that will help them function effectively. These **norms** include:

1. I don't have to be perfect and neither do you!

# Table 6:1
# CSG's And Traditional Teams

## Colleagial Support Group  Traditional Team

| Colleagial Support Group | Traditional Team |
|---|---|
| Clear positive interdependence is structured among teachers | Teachers are told to work together |
| Regular face-to-face interaction | Teachers often work independently |
| High individual accountability | No individual accountability |
| Teachers are trained in interpersonal and small group skills | No skill training is provided |
| All members share leadership responsibilities | A team leader is assigned |
| Teachers process how effectively their group is functioning | No group processing |

2. It takes time to master cooperative learning procedures to a routine use level.

3. I'm here to improve my competence in using cooperative learning procedures.

4. You can criticize my implementation of cooperative learning procedures without me taking it personally.

5. I am secure enough to give you feedback about your implementation of cooperative learning procedures.

# Structuring Colleagial Support Groups

There are a number of steps that "cooperative learning leaders" need to go through in structuring and managing colleagial support groups aimed at implementing cooperative learning procedures in the classroom. These steps include:

1. Publicly announce your support for the use of cooperative learning procedures.

2. Recruit and select competent teachers to participate in the colleagial support groups.

3. Inform them of (or review with them) the nature of cooperative learning.

4. Highlight the goal interdependence among members of a colleagial support group.

5. Negotiate a contract among the members of the colleagial support groups and a contract between the groups and you, if appropriate.

6. Structure the first few meetings of the colleagial support group until members are able to structure them by themselves.

7. Provide the resources and incentives needed for the colleagial support groups to function.

8. Ensure that the colleagial support groups discuss how well they function and maintain good relationships among members.

9. Build yourself in as a member not out as a consultant.

10. Keep a long-term, developmental perspective and protect the colleagial support groups from other pressures.

Each of these steps will be discussed in the following sections.

## Announcing Your Support

Forming of teacher colleagial support groups, aimed at improving competencies in using cooperative learning procedures, begins with the "cooperative learning leaders" announcing their support for teachers using cooperative learning strategies. This should take place on important occasions such as beginning staff meetings. Such announcements should be frequent and cooperative learning should be described concretely in terms of life in school. The teachers who are using cooperative learning procedures should be visibly and publicly praised. The message that should be given is, "It is proper to structure learning cooperatively and therefore the staff should strive to do so." During the year, give updates on new research or describe new procedures to implement cooperative learning. Describe how cooperative learning agrees with district and school goals. Tolerate and absorb any initial failures of teachers learning how to structure lessons cooperatively. It is important that supervisors or principals do not kill cooperative learning by skepticism or neglect.

## Recruiting Teachers

Teachers can be recruited or selected to participate in colleagial support groups in a number of ways. You will want to look for members who are open, sensitive, supportive, and colleagially competent. Disgruntled, nonconstructive teachers tend to ruin colleagial support groups. Their criticism is rarely productive and they often lack wisdom in choosing battle-grounds. Alienated teachers may also be disruptive and demoralizing. And incompetent teachers who are struggling to survive are unprepared to begin professional growth until they gain basic control and self-confidence. Also, the members should be hand-picked to make sure the colleagial support groups are successful.

## Reviewing the Nature of Cooperative Learning

When you have established the membership of a colleagial support group, you will find it helpful to review the nature of cooperative learning for the members. **Methods** are:

1. Recommend a training course or workshop they can participate in.

2. Arrange for them to observe a teacher who is highly experienced in using cooperative learning procedures.

3. Provide reading material on cooperative learning.

4. Have consultants or experienced teachers present an awareness session for all the staff in the school.

5. Have the group meet with a district specialist in cooperative learning.

## Highlighting Goal Interdependence

The basic goal of a colleagial support group is to work jointly to improve continuously each other's competence in using cooperative learning procedures or, in other words, to teach each other how to better use cooperative learning strategies. **The fact that the members of a colleagial support group "sink or swim together" needs to be made quite clear to all members.**

## Negotiating the Two Contracts

**When teachers become part of a colleagial support group they accept certain mutual responsibilities.** These include:

1. To attend the meetings of the colleagial support group.

2. To commit themselves to increasing their competence in using cooperative learning procedures.

3. To commit themselves to helping other members increase their competence in using cooperative learning procedures.

4. To discuss their use of cooperative learning procedures and engage in problem-solving to improve the implementation efforts of themselves and the other members.

5. To share the work of including cooperative learning in existing curriculum materials with the other members of the group.

6. To ask other members to observe periodically as they teach cooperatively structured lessons and to provide them with feedback.

7. To agree to observe the other members teach cooperatively structured lessons and to provide them with feedback.

8. To contribute constructively to the goal achievement of the colleagial support group and to maintain high quality working relationships among members.

These responsibilities need to be made into a contract that is eventually formalized and will serve as a basis for discussing how well the colleagial support group is functioning. The responsibilities of the "cooperative learning leaders" in structuring and managing the colleagial support group need to be clear in order to legitimize their involvement in the group. For instance, the group is not a place for teachers to evaluate each other, and this should be made clear to the group members.

## Structuring the Initial Meetings

**The activities of the colleagial support group are aimed at helping all members master, refine, adapt, and experiment with cooperative learning procedures.** Discussing their implementation efforts, jointly planning lessons and jointly designing curriculum materials, and reciprocally observing each other's implementation efforts are the major activities of the group.

The "cooperative learning leader" should schedule and convene the **first meeting of the colleagial support group** and ensure that it covers the following agenda items:

1. Your support of their efforts in implementing cooperative learning procedures.

2. When the regular meeting time will be. The meeting has to last at least 50 to 60 minutes. Breakfast clubs, which meet

once a week for breakfast before school begins are popular.

3. The purposes of meetings (discussion of implementation efforts, joint planning of lessons and materials, and reciprocal observation).

4. An assessment of the resources they need in order to meet regularly and engage in these activities. Potential resources are discussed in the next section.

5. Plans to make each meeting both productive and fun. With that in mind you might ask who is going to be in charge of the refreshments for the next meeting (a cooperative effort is recommended).

6. Specific plans for:

   a. When the next meeting will be.

   b. What cooperatively structured lessons they will teach before the next meeting.

   c. What the agenda for the next meeting will be (one item will be to discuss how well their cooperatively structured lessons went).

7. Agree on a tentative contract among members and between the group and yourself.

**A sample agenda for the second meeting is:**

1. Welcome everyone and have a "warm-up," such as a handout on the types of positive interdependence that may be used in cooperatively structured lessons.

2. Discuss their use of cooperative learning procedures:

   a. Lessons taught during the past week.

   b. Their successes--what were the things they liked best.

   c.  Any problems that surfaced during the lessons.

3. Discuss the problems at some length and generate a number of alternative strategies for solving each, so that each member may select from a menu of alternative solutions rather than having to implement any one solution.

4. Jointly plan a lesson that they will all teach during the following week.

5. Plan the agenda and menu for the next meeting.

**A sample agenda for the third meeting may be:**

1. Warm up by handing out a list of ways of ensuring individual accountability in cooperatively structured lessons.

2. Discussing how well the lesson they taught went, identifying positive aspects and problems that arose.

3. Discuss the problems and generate a number of solutions that might be implemented. Revise the lesson to solve any problems.

4. Plan for as many of the members as possible to observe each other teach a lesson structured cooperatively during the following week. Make specific contracts as to what the observer should focus on. An outline of the teacher's role in cooperative learning situations may be helpful.

5. Set agenda and menu for the following week.

**The sample agenda for the fourth meeting is as follows:**

1. Warm up by handing out material on teaching students the social skills they need to work collaboratively.

2. Discuss how well the observations went and what the members observed. The roles for constructive feedback should be reviewed (see Johnson, 1986). The basic components of cooperative learning situations should also be reviewed.

Your role is to ensure that all feedback is constructive and helpful.

3. Plan for the next round of observations.

4. Set the agenda and the menu for the next meeting.

These sample agendas are only aimed at outlining what might happen in the initial meetings of the colleagial support groups. You will need to revise these meeting agendas to better meet the needs of your teachers.

## Providing Resources and Incentives

Teachers' perceptions of their interdependence may be considerably enhanced if you offer joint incentives for being an effective colleagial support group. Incentives can be classified as tangible, interpersonal, and personal. Some examples of incentives teachers find valuable are:

1. The opportunity to present an inservice session on cooperative learning procedures to the other members of the staff or to the staff of another school.

2. The opportunity to apply for summer salaries to revise curriculum for cooperatively structured lessons.

3. Visible public praise for their efforts in implementing cooperative learning procedures.

4. Written recognition of their efforts which goes into their individual files.

5. The opportunity to observe teachers in other schools implementing cooperative learning procedures.

The more tangible the group incentives offered, the greater the perceived interdependence among teachers. A maxim developed within the business/industrial sector of our society states, "If two individuals get paid for working as a pair, it is amazing how much interest they take in helping one another succeed!"

**To be effective, a colleagial support group will need a variety of resources that only supervisors and principals can provide.** Needed resources include:

1. Released time during working hours to meet.

2. A small fund for materials and expenses in implementing cooperative learning.

3. Released time to observe each other teach cooperative lessons.

4. Released time to visit the classrooms of teachers in other schools who are experienced in using cooperative learning procedures.

5. Materials on cooperative learning, such as research updates, helpful hints, sample lesson plans, books, and so forth.

6. Your time and resources to help them get started and to help them maintain high interest and involvement in implementing cooperative learning procedures in their classrooms.

7. Your emotional support and encouragement to continue their efforts. Always remember that pressure (however subtle) on teachers to implement cooperative learning procedures in their classrooms must be coupled with tangible and visible support from you.

## Discussing How Well the Professional Support Groups Function

One area in which most teacher colleagial support groups need considerable help and encouragement is in discussing how well their meetings are contributing to achieving the group's goals and to maintaining effective working relationships among members. This means that you will need to take some initiative in ensuring that one teacher periodically systematically observes a meeting and time is spent on processing how well the group is functioning. After the teachers become experienced in helping their student groups discuss their group functioning, the teachers' abilities to discuss the functioning of their own meetings should increase. But even the most experienced teachers may avoid discussing the functioning of meetings unless the supervisors or principals structure it.

## Building Yourself In As a Member

You should be part of each colleagial support group in your jurisdiction. Build yourself in not out! Do not be lonely! Members of a colleagial support group will enjoy considerable success, feel a sense of accomplishment, like each other, see each other as supportive and accepting, and have a sense of camaraderie that significantly increases the quality of their colleagial lives. You should be part of these feelings!

## Protecting and Nurturing

When teachers become serious about implementing cooperative learning procedures in their classrooms, supervisors and principals will have to do a number of things to protect and nurture the teachers' efforts. Some examples are:

1. There will inevitably be initial failures and problems. Students may be unhappy about the change in the "system," students will be unskilled in working collaboratively, materials may be inappropriate, and what a teacher may define as cooperative learning may not be what you define as cooperative learning. You will have to allow for these initial problems and communicate strongly to your teachers that such initial "start-up costs" are to be expected and accepted. Do not require your teachers to be perfect during the first week they try structuring lessons cooperatively!

2. There will be other innovations within your jurisdiction that will compete for teachers' attention and energy. Part of your responsibilities are to find commonalties of interest

and intent among presumably opposing innovations. Encourage your teachers to integrate cooperative learning with other instructional strategies they use or are trying out. But at all costs avoid the cycle of making cooperative learning the focus for a few months or a year and then springing another innovation on your teachers. The "try it and then drop it for the next fad" cycle is especially destructive to quality teaching. Make sure that your teachers recognize that your and their commitment to cooperative learning has to span a number of years.

3. Translate what cooperative learning is so that diverse groups of teachers can understand its importance and usefulness.

4. Deflect, soften, and negate resistance to implementing cooperative learning within your staff. If some teachers believe "I tried that once and it did not work," protect the teachers who are willing to become involved in implement-ing cooperative learning in their classrooms from demoralizing conversations and criticism from such colleagues.

5. Within any staff there may be destructive competition among teachers as to who is best. Part of your responsibilities are to defuse such "win-lose" dynamics and encourage mutual respect, support, and assistance among your teachers.

6. Within any colleagial support group there will come a time when one member has hurt the feelings of another member or when conflicts arise that disrupt the cohesiveness and productivity of the group. Your task at that point is to ensure that hurt feelings become repaired and that conflicts are constructively resolved. For specific procedures for doing so, see Johnson and Johnson (1987b).

7. Most teachers are concerned that, if a parent complains about their use of cooperative learning procedures, they will receive strong support from their principal and supervisors. Give it. If the parents of the students are con-

cerned and involved in their children's education, they may be curious or even skeptical at any modification of teaching procedures. Be ready to explain why a teacher is using cooperative learning procedures and that it is with your full support and approval.

8. Have the courage to see your teachers through the process of learning how to use cooperative learning procedures effectively.

## Thinking Developmentally

Mastering cooperative learning procedures so that they are used routinely takes time. For most teachers it does not happen in a few weeks or even in a few months. You should always think in terms of development, not in radically changing everything the teacher is doing immediately. Start with one area, perfect your procedures, and then expand to a second area. Plan developmentally for a two or three year process with heavy emphasis on supporting and maintaining interest.

# A District Strategy

General procedures "cooperative learning leaders" may use in institutionalizing cooperative learning within their school district are as follows:

1. Give a general awareness inservice session to an entire school and ask for volunteers to become a school-based colleagial support group to work systematically on improving their skills in using cooperative learning procedures.

2. Give the basic training in cooperative learning, using this book to ensure that all the critical aspects are covered systematically.

3. Work with each teacher individually:

a. Teach a cooperatively structured lesson in his or her classroom.

b. Co-plan a cooperatively structured lesson which is then jointly taught.

c. Co-plan a lesson that the teacher teaches while you observe.

Through repeated classroom visits each teacher should be trained one-on-one. Some basic rules for working with an individual teacher are:

a. All lessons are prepared together.

b. The teacher is the expert on his or her classroom while you are the expert on cooperative learning.

c. When you are in the teacher's classroom, the teacher owns the lesson. It is the teacher's lesson, not yours.

d. Each time you meet with a teacher have some new helpful strategy, activity, or set of materials that is tailored to the teacher's subject area or to a specific problem student in the teacher's classroom. This builds a personal as well as a colleagial aspect to the help and assistance in implementing cooperative learning procedures.

4. Network the teachers you are training into colleagial support groups. These groups may meet with and without you.

5. As an additional maintenance procedure, each month send out a newsletter on "How to Help Students Work in Groups." The newsletter contains lesson plans and classroom activities that teachers can try out and/or discuss in the meetings of their colleagial support groups.

6. Meet regularly with curriculum directors, talk to parent groups, attend the principals' cabinet meetings, trouble-shoot for your teachers, coordinate collaboration among support group members, and generally spend your days in schools and classrooms.

7. Be genuinely enthusiastic about the use of cooperative learning procedures. Build personal and supportive relationships with the teachers you work with, and show in-genuity in discovering ways to help teachers use coopera-tive learning procedures.

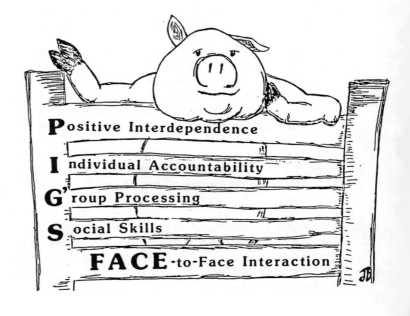

Positive Interdependence

Individual Accountability

Group Processing

Social Skills

FACE-to-Face Interaction

# Chapter Seven:

# Myths About Cooperative Learning

## Introduction

Among the questions repeatedly asked by teachers and administrators during training sessions on cooperative learning, some come from untrue assumptions about how school ought to be and what students should be trained to do. This chapter discusses these often asked questions and explores a few myths about schools and teaching.

## Myth 1: Schools Should Emphasize Competition Because It's A Dog-Eat-Dog World

Not true. It is a person-help-person world. When you look closely, you will find that it is almost all human activity is cooperative. We speak a common language, we have a set of laws governing our actions, we work in an economic system characterized by an elaborate division of labor, and we live in families and communities held together by our common interests. Like all social systems, our educational system is based on coordinating the actions of millions of individuals to achieve mutual goals. We live in an interdependent world. It goes on and on. Giraffes have survived as a species because of their long necks, cheetahs because of their speed, and humans because of our ability to cooperate to achieve mutual goals. Cooperation is such an integral part of human existence that, like a fish trying to be aware of water, we only know it's there when it breaks down.

To make school life more realistic, classrooms should be dominated by cooperative learning activities. This does not, however, mean that students should not learn how to compete appropriately for fun and enjoyment, win or lose. When the overall context is cooperative, competition provides an interesting and enjoyable change of pace without students believing that winning is a life or death matter. We also believe that some individualistic work, where students work autonomously and take responsibility to follow through on a task, is essential. Cooperatively-structured lessons should both prepare students to do similar work alone and provide a setting in which individual accomplishments and competencies are used to contribute to the overall achievement of the group. We would be very disappointed to see **only** cooperative learning being used within a classroom, but we are pragmatic enough to recognize that cooperation is the key to an effective classroom learning climate.

## Myth 2: High-Achieving Students Are Penalized by Working In Heterogeneous Cooperative Learning Groups

To most educators it is obvious that low- and middle-achieving students have much to gain by working in cooperative learning groups with high-achieving peers. In terms of both motivation and actual achievement the largest gainers from working in heterogeneous cooperative learning groups are the struggling, low-achieving students and the next largest gainers are the mid-dle-achievers.

What is not so obvious to many educators is that high-achieving students benefit in a number of ways from collaborating with low- and middle-achieving peers. We and others around the country have conducted numerous studies comparing the achievement of high-, middle-, and low-achieving students in cooperative, competitive, and individualistic learning situations. The high-achievers working in heterogeneous cooperative groups have never done worse than their counterparts working competitively or individualistically, and often they do better. When the research investigates other aspects of achievement than score on a test the benefits for high-achieving students become more apparent. High-achieving students working in heterogeneous learning groups score higher on retention tests than do high-achievers who participated in competitive or individualistic learning situations. The quality of reasoning strategies used by the high-achievers was higher when they were in cooperative learning situations. The cognitive processes involved in having to talk through and explain (perhaps in several different ways) the material being studied seems to enhance retention and promote the development of higher-level reasoning strategies. It may be that bright students get quick, intuitive, right answers to problems, but may not have a conscious strategy for getting the answer. There is growing evidence that a silent student is a student who is not engaging in the cognitive processes necessary for high- quality learning.

An equally important benefit for high-achievers participating in heterogeneous cooperative learning groups is the development of collaborative skills and friendships that result. While bright students are often resented and sometimes ostracized in a competitive setting, they are seen as desirable partners in a cooperative setting. And in collaborating with middle- and low- achieving peers (as well as other bright students) high-achievers are more likely to develop the leadership, communication, decision-making, and conflict management skills they need for future career success.

# Myth 3: Every Member Of A Cooperative Learning Group Has To Do The Same Work And Proceed At The Same Rate

When mainstreaming academically handicapped students into the regular classroom, many educators believe that cooperative learning procedures are not possible because the handicapped students cannot do work on the same level and at the same speed as the other students in the class. There are many important advantages for having handicapped students collaborating with nonhandicapped peers and vise versa. The impact on collaborative skills, friendships, appreciation of human diversity, perspective-taking ability, and quality of life is considerable.

Each student in a cooperative learning group can be given different material to learn. In a spelling group, for example, each student can have a different set of words and/or a different number of words to learn. In a math class each group member can have a different set of problems and/or a different number of problems to solve. Academically handicapped students may be evaluated according to different criteria so that the other group members are not penalized. Members of the same learning group can discuss, edit, check, and correct each other's work without working on the same material or at the same speed.

# Myth 4: A Single Group Grade Shared By Group Members Is Not Fair

Having students work together on a joint product is viewed by many educators as being less fair to each student than is having each student work alone to produce an individual product for which he or she receives an individual grade. Most students would disagree. It is important that students perceive the distribution of grades and other rewards as being fair, otherwise they may become unmotivated and withdraw psychologically or physically. There have been a number of investigations of students' views of the fairness of various grading systems. There are five major findings:

1. Students who "lose" in a competitive learning situation commonly perceive the grading system as being unjust and, consequently, dislike the class and the teacher (Johnson & Johnson, 1983, in press).

2. Before a task is performed, students generally perceive a competitive grading system as being the most fair, but after a task is completed, having all members receive the same grade or reward is viewed as the fairest (Deutsch, 1979).

3. The more frequently students have experienced long-term cooperative learning experiences, and the more cooperative learning was used in their classes, then the more the students believed that everyone who tries has an equal chance to succeed in class, that students get the grades they deserve, and that the grading system is fair (Johnson & Johnson, 1983).

4. Students who have experienced cooperative learning prefer group grades over individual ones (Wheeler & Ryan, 1973).

5. Achievement is higher when group grades (compared with individual ones) are given (Johnson & Johnson, in press). The implications of this research for teachers is that group grades may be perceived to be unfair by students before the students have participated in a cooperative learning activity. Once cooperation has been experienced for a while, however, a single group grade will probably be perceived as the fairest method of evaluation.

There are three general systems for distributing rewards within our society: **equity** (where the person who contributed the most or scored the highest receives the greatest reward), **equality** (where every participant receives the same reward), and **need** (where those who have the greatest need receive the greatest reward) (Deutsch, 1975). All three systems operate within our society and all three systems have their ethical rationale. Typically, the equality system assures members of a family, community, organization, or society that their basic needs will be met and that diverse contributions will be equally valued. The need system assures members that in moments of crisis others will provide support and assistance. And the equity system assures members that if they strive for excellence, their contributions will be valued and rewarded. Educators who wish to give rewards in the classroom only on the basis of equity may be viewing "fairness" from too limited a perspective.

In the ideal classroom, at the end of a grading period, each student will have a number of grades resulting from collaborative efforts, a number of grades resulting from individualistic efforts, and a number of grades resulting from competitive efforts. When these grades are added together, teachers we have worked with inevitably find that high-achievers get "A's." Because of the higher achievement found in cooperative learning situations, however, middle- and low-achievers may receive higher grades than they would if the classroom was dominated by competitive or individualistic learning situations. The number of students receiving "B's" and "C's" will tend to grow larger as the positive peer pressure and support raise achievement. The number of "D's" and "F's" will tend to disappear as collaborators refuse to allow unmotivated students to stay that way. In order not to undermine the overall class collaborativeness it is important to use a criterion-referenced evaluation system in determining final grades.

For teachers who want to give individual grades within cooperative learning situations there are a number of alternatives that have been successfully used:

1. **Bonus point method:** Students work together in cooperative learning groups, prepare each other for the test, take the test individually, and receive an individual grade. If all members of their group, however, achieve up to a preset criterion of excellence, then each member is rewarded bonus points.

2. **Dual grading system**: Students work together in cooperative learning groups, prepare each other for the test, take the test individually, and receive an individual grade. They then receive a second grade based on the total performance of all group members.

3. **Alternative reward**: Same as "2" except that the group grade is used to determine whether group members receive a nonacademic reward, such as free-time, extra recess time, or popcorn.

A science teacher in Austin, Texas, uses a grading system we like. Students work in cooperative learning groups during the week. The students take a weekly examination individually and their score becomes their base score. They then receive 5 bonus points if all group members score above 60 percent on the test. This encourages intergroup cooperation. His latest addition to the system is to give another 5 bonus points to every student if all students in the five science classes score above 60 percent on the test. This encourages cooperation across classes. We have a mental image of students going through the hall asking others, "Are you taking science? Take your book home and study!"

# Myth 5: Using Cooperative Learning Is Simple

Wrong! Cooperative learning is important for increasing the quality of life within the classroom, students' achievement and critical thinking ability, and students' long-term well-being and success. But it is not easy or simple to implement. The concept of cooperation is simple. But switching a classroom from an emphasis on individualistic and competitive learning to a classroom dominated by collaboration is a complex and long-term process.

Learning how to structure learning situations cooperatively is much like peeling an onion. The teacher learns how to structure productive cooperative learning activities layer after layer until the heart is reached. Over a period of years of using cooperation the learning experiences become richer and richer. The layers include: learning how to place students in productive groups and structuring cooperative learning goals, monitoring and intervening to improve students' collaborative skills, directly teaching students cooperative skills, experimenting with various ways of arranging curriculum materials to promote positive interdependence, promoting academic controversies within the cooperative learning groups, and finally, the integration of cooperative learning activities with competitive and individualistic learning activities. There is nothing simple in such a process. But the results are worth it.

## Myth 6: The Schools Can Change Overnight

Wrong again! Fads come and go quickly, but transforming classrooms to become places where students care about each other's learning and work cooperatively takes time. Where cooperative learning is concerned, we have always believed more in "evolution" than "revolution" where cooperative learning was concerned. Cooperative learning has been implemented differently in different school districts, but all the successful implementations have evolved over a period of time and have provided teachers with ongoing support. Consider the following example.

## Summary

Remember, it's a people-help-people world; all students, including high-achievers, benefit from participating in heterogeneous cooperative learning groups; different assignments may be given to different members of a cooperative learning group when it is desirable to do so; when teachers wish to do so, group grades may be given and will be perceived as fair by most students; mastering cooperative learning strategies is difficult; and cooperative learning procedures have a richness that takes a teacher several years to explore.

# Chapter 8

# Where You Go From Here

## Types Of Cooperative Learning

The previous chapters in this book have carefully described the use of formal cooperative learning groups. After mastering the use of formal cooperative learning groups, you may wish to add informal cooperative learning groups, and cooperative base groups (Johnson, Johnson, & Holubec, 1988b).

### Formal Cooperative Learning Groups

**Formal cooperative learning groups** may last for several minutes to several class sessions to complete a specific task or assignment (such as solving a set of problems, completing a unit, writing a report or theme, conducting an experiment, and reading and comprehending a story, play, chapter, or book). This book has focused on formal cooperative learning groups. Any course requirement or assignment may be reformulated to be cooperative rather than competitive or individualistic through the use of formal cooperative learning groups. **Gaining expertise in using formal cooperative learning groups provides the foundation for gaining expertise in using informal and base groups.**

### Informal Cooperative Learning Groups

**Informal cooperative learning groups** are temporary, ad hoc groups that last for only one discussion or one class period. Their **purposes** are to focus student attention on the material to be learned, create an expectation set and mood conducive to learning, help organize in advance the material to be covered in a class session, ensure that students cognitively process the material being taught, and provide closure to an instructional session. They may be used at any time, but are especially useful during a lecture or direct teaching. The length of time students can attend to a lecture before their minds drift away is estimated to be from 12 to 15 minutes.

**During direct teaching the instructional challenge for the teacher is to ensure that students do the intellectual work of organizing material, explaining it, summarizing it, and integrating it into existing conceptual networks.** This may be achieved by having students do the advance organizing, cognitive process what they are learning, and provide closure to the lesson. Breaking up lectures with short cooperative processing times will give you less lecture time, but will enhance what is learned and build relationships among the students in your class. It will help counter what is proclaimed as the main problem of lectures: "The information passes from the notes of the teacher to the notes of the student without passing through the mind of either one."

The following procedure may help to plan a lecture that keeps students actively engaged intellectually. It entails having **focused discussions** before and after a lecture (i.e., bookends) and interspersing **turn-to-your-partner** discussions throughout the lecture.

1. **Focused Discussion 1**: Plan your lecture around a series of questions that the lecture answers. Prepare the questions on an overhead transparency or write them on the board so that students can see them. Students will discuss the questions in pairs. The discussion task is aimed at promoting **advance organizing** of what the students know about the topic to be presented and creates an **expectation set** and a learning mood conductive to learning.

2. **Turn-To-Your-Partner Discussions**: Divide the lecture into 10 to 15 minute segments. Plan a short discussion task to be given to pairs of students after each segment. The task

needs to be short enough that students can complete it within three or four minutes. Its purpose is to ensure that students are actively thinking about the material being presented. **It is important that students are randomly called on to share their answers after each discussion task.** Such **individual accountability** ensures that the pairs take the tasks seriously and check each other to ensure that both are prepared to answer. Each discussion task should have four components: **formulate** an answer to the question being asked, **share** your answer with your partner, **listen** carefully to his or her answer, and to **create** a new answer that is superior to each member's initial formulation through the processes of association, building on each other's thoughts, and synthesizing. Students will need to gain some experience with this procedure to become skilled in doing it within a short period of time.

3. **Focused Discussion 2:** Give students an ending discussion task to provide closure to the lecture. Usually students are given five or six minutes to summarize and discuss the material covered in the lecture. The discussion should result in students integrating what they have just learned into existing conceptual frameworks. The task may also point students toward what the homework will cover or what will be presented in the next class session.

Until students become familiar and experienced with the procedure, **process** it regularly to help them increase their skill and speed in completing short discussion tasks.

The informal cooperative learning group is not only effective for getting students actively involved in processing what they are learning, it also provides time for you to gather your wits, reorganize your notes, take a deep breath, and move around the class listening to what students are saying. Listening to student discussions provides you with "windows" into your students' levels of reasoning and gives you direction and insight into how the concepts you are teaching are being grasped by your students.

## Base Groups

**Base groups** are long-term, heterogeneous cooperative learning groups with stable membership. **The primary responsibility of members is to provide each other with the support, encouragement, and assistance they need to make academic progress.** The base group verifies that each member is completing the assignments and progressing satisfactory through the academic program. Base groups may be given the task of letting absent group members know what went on in the class when they miss a session and bring them up to date. The use of base groups tends to improve attendance, personalize the work required and the school experience, and improve the quality and quantity of learning. The base group is the source of permanent and caring peer relationships within which students are committed to and support each other's educational success.

Base groups last for at least a semester or year and preferably for several years. The larger the class and the more complex the subject matter, the more important it is to have base groups. Learning for your groupmates is a powerful motivator. Receiving social support and being held accountable for appropriate behavior by peers who care about you and have a long-term commitment to your success and well-being is an important aspect of growing up and progressing through school.

**It is important that some of the relationships built within cooperative learning groups are permanent.** School has to be more than a series of "ship-board romances" that last for only a semester or year. In elementary, junior-high, high-schools, and colleges students should be assigned to permanent base groups. The base groups should then be assigned to most classes so that members spend much of the day together and regularly complete cooperative learning tasks. Doing so can create permanent caring and committed relationships that will provide students with the support, help, encouragement, and assistance they need to make academic progress and develop cognitively and socially in healthy ways.

When used in combination, these formal, informal, and base cooperative learning groups provide an overall structure to classroom life. The use of informal and base groups are described in depth in **Advanced cooperative learning** by Johnson, Johnson, and Holubec (1988).

# Teaching Students' Social Skills

An important part of your expertise in using cooperative learning is to teach students additional social skills. There are many sources of further social skills to be taught to students, including **Advanced Cooperative Learning** (Johnson, Johnson, & Holubec, 1988b), **Reaching Out** (Johnson, 1990), and **Joining Together** (Johnson & F. Johnson, 1987).

# Integrated Use Of All Three Goal Structures

Another way to increase your expertise in using cooperative learning is to use all three goal structures within an integrated way. While the dominant goal structure within any classroom should be cooperation (which ideally would be used about 60 - 70 percent of the time), competitive and individualistic efforts are useful supplements. Competition may be used as a fun change-of-pace during an instructional unit that is predominantly structured cooperatively and individualistic learning is often productive when the information learned is subsequently used in a cooperative activity. The integrated use of cooperative, competitive, and individualistic learning is described in depth with in Johnson and Johnson (1987a) and Johnson, Johnson, and Holubec (1988).

# Utilizing Creative Conflict

When cooperative learning is established in your classroom, you may wish to promote the creative use of conflict. Teachers are peacemakers. Much of their time is spent dealing with conflicts among students, between students and staff, between staff and parents, or even among staff members. Conflicts are inevitable whenever committed people work together to achieve mutual goals. Whether the conflicts are constructive influences that promote greater productivity and closer personal relationships, or destructive influences that create divisiveness and ineffectiveness, depends on how they are managed.

Conflicts are constructively managed through a five step procedure of (Johnson & Johnson, 1987). **The first step is creating a cooperative context.** In order for long-term mutual interests to be recognized and valued, individuals have to perceive their interdependence and be invested in each other's well being. **The second step is structuring academic controversies.** In order to maximize student achievement, critical thinking, and higher-level reasoning, students need to engage in intellectual conflicts. Within structured controversies, students work with a learning partner in examining an academic issue, preparing a pro or con position, advocating their position to an opposing pair, criticizing the opposing position, reversing perspectives, and synthesizing the best arguments on both sides to derive a conclusion. The use of academic controversy is a very powerful instructional procedure that will move cooperative learning groups to new heights of productivity and higher-level learning.

**The third step is teaching students how to negotiate and the fourth step is teaching students how to mediate.** Students first try to negotiate their conflicts and, if that fails, ask a mediator for help. Finally, when mediation fails, **the teacher or principal arbitrates the conflict.** This is a last resort because it typically involves deciding who is right and wrong, leaving at least one student angry toward the arbitrator.

The procedures for using this five-step process of utilizing constructive conflict to improve instruction may be found in **Creative Conflict** by Johnson and Johnson (1987).

# Empowering Staff Through Cooperative Teams

What is good for students is even better for staff. **A cooperative school is one in which cooperative learning dominates classroom and cooperative teams dominate staff efforts.** It is social support from and accountability to valued peers that motivates committed efforts to succeed. Empowering staff members through cooperative teamwork is done in three ways: (1) **colleagial support groups** (to increase teachers' instructional expertise and success), (2) **task forces** (to plan and implement solutions to school-wide issues and problems such as curriculum adoptions and lunchroom behavior), and (3) **ad hoc decision-making groups** (to are used during faculty meetings to involve all staff members in important school decisions). How to structure and use these three types of cooperative teams may be found in **Leading the cooperative school** by Johnson and Johnson (1989).

# Looking Forward

At the end of this book you are at a new beginning. Years of experience in using cooperative learning in your classroom are needed to gain expertise in its use. While you are using cooperative learning there is much more to learn about its use. The addition of informal cooperative learning activities and long-term permanent base groups will increase the power and effectiveness of cooperation in your classroom. Teaching students more and more sophisticated social skills will improve how well they work together to maximize their learning. Supplementing the use of cooperative learning with appropriate competitions and individualistic assignments will further enrich the quality of learning within your classroom. Structuring academic controversies within your cooperative learning groups will move students to higher levels of reasoning and thinking while providing a considerable increase in energy and fun. Teaching students how to negotiate their differences and mediate each other's conflicts will accelerate their skills in managing conflicts within cooperative learning groups. Finally, moving cooperation up to the school and district levels by structuring staff into cooperative teams will create a congruent organizational structure within which both faculty and students will thrive.

# References

Anderson, L. (1984). What teachers don't do and why. **Educational Report, 27,** 1 & 4, University of South Carolina.

**Belonging** (16 mm film) (1980). Edina, MN: Interaction Book Company.

Berman, P., & McLaughlin, M. (1978). **Federal programs supporting educational change, Vol. VIII: Implementing and sustaining innovations.** Santa Monica, CA: Rand Corporation.

Blake, R., & Moulton, J. (1961). Comprehension of own and out-group positions under intergroup competition. **Journal of Conflict Resolution, 5,** 304-310.

Bower, S. (1960). **Early identification of emotionally handicapped children in school.** Springfield, IL: Thomas.

Campbell, J. (1965). **The children's crusader: Colonel Francis W. Parker.** PhD dissertation, Teachers College, Columbia University.

**Circles of Learning** (16mm film)(1983). Edina, MN: Interaction Book Company.

Cohen, E. (1986). **Designing groupwork.** New York: Teachers College Press.

Crawford, J., & Haaland, G. (1972). Predecisional information seeking and subsequent conformity in the social influence process. **Journal of Personality and Social Psychology, 23,** 112- 119.

Deutsch, M. (1949). An experimental study of the effects of cooperation and competition upon group processes. **Human Relations, 2**, 199-232.

Deutsch, M. (1962). Cooperation and trust: Some theoretical notes. In M. Jones (Ed.), **Nebraska symposium on motivation,** 275- 319. Lincoln, NE: University of Nebraska Press.

Deutsch, M. (1973). **The resolution of conflict.** New Haven, CT: Yale University Press.

Deutsch, M. (1975). Equity, equality, and need: What determines which values will be used as the basis for distributive justice. **Journal of Social Issues, 31**, 137-149.

DeVries, D., & Edwards, K. (1974). Student teams and learning games: Their effects on cross-race and cross-sex interaction. **Journal of Educational Psychology, 66,** 741-749.

Dishon, D., & O'Leary, P. (1984). **A guidebook for cooperative learning**. Holmes Beach, FL: Learning Publications.

Goodlad, J. (1983). **A place called school.** New York: McGraw-Hill.

Glasser, W. (1986). **Control theory in the classroom**. New York: Harper & Row.

Harkins, S., & Petty, R. (1982). The effects of task difficulty and task uniqueness on social loafing. **Journal of Personality and Social Psychology, 43,** 1214-1229.

Hartup, W. (1976). Peer interaction and the behavioral development of the individual child. In E. Schloper & R. Reicher (Eds.), **Psychopathology and child development.** New York: Plenum Press.

Ingham, A., Levinger, G., Graves, J., & Peckham, V. (1974). The Ringelmann effect: Studies of group size and group performance. **Journal of Personality and Social Psychology, 10,** 371-384.

Johnson, D. W. (1979). **Educational psychology.** Englewood Cliffs, NJ: Prentice-Hall.

Johnson, D. W. (1980). Constructive peer relationships, social development, and cooperative learning experiences: Implications for the preventino of drug abuse. **Journal of Drug Education**, 10, 7.24.

Johnson, D. W. (1987). **Human relations and your career** (2nd ed.). Englewood Cliffs, NJ: Prentice-Hall.

Johnson, D. W. (1990). **Reaching out: Interpersonal effectiveness and self-actualization.** (4th ed.). Englewood Cliffs, NJ: Prentice-Hall.

Johnson, D. W., & Johnson, F. (1987). **Joining together: Group theory and group skills** (3rd ed.). Englewood Cliffs, NJ: Prentice-Hall.

Johnson, D. W., & Johnson, R. (1974). Instructional goal structure: Cooperative, competitive, or individualistic. **Review of Educational Research, 44,** 213-240.

Johnson, D. W., & Johnson, R. (1976). Students' perceptions of and preferences for cooperative and competitive learning experiences. **Perceptual and Motor Skills, 42,** 989-990.

Johnson, D. W., & Johnson, R. (Eds.), (1978). Social interdependence within instruction. **Journal of Research and Development in Education, 12**(1).

Johnson, D. W., & Johnson, R. (1979). Conflict in the classroom: Controversy and learning. **Review of Educational Research, 49,** 51-70.

Johnson, D. W., & Johnson, R. (1980). Integrating handicapped students into the mainstream. **Exceptional Children, 46,** 89-98.

Johnson, D. W., & Johnson, R. (1982). Healthy peer relationships: A necessity not a luxury. In P. Roy (Ed.), **Structuring**

**cooperative learning: The 1982 handbook**. Edina, MN: Interaction Book Company.

Johnson, D. W., & Johnson, R. (1982). Effects of cooperative and individualistic instruction on handicapped and nonhandicapped students. **Journal of Social Psychology, 118,** 257-268.

Johnson, D. W., & Johnson, R. (1983). The socialization and achievement crisis: Are cooperative learning experiences the solution? In L. Bickman (Ed.), **Applied social psychology annual 4.** Beverly Hills, CA: Sage Publishing.

Johnson, D. W., & Johnson, R. (1987a). **Learning together and alone: Cooperation, competition, and individualistic learning** (2nd ed.). Englewood Cliffs, NJ: Prentice-Hall.

Johnson, D. W., & Johnson, R. (1987b). **Creative Conflict.** Edina, MN: Interaction Book Company.

Johnson, D. W., & Johnson, R. (1989a). **Cooperation and competition: Theory and research.** Edina, MN: Interaction Book Company.

Johnson, D. W., & Johnson, R. (1989b). **Leading the cooperative school.** Edina, MN: Interaction Book Company.

Johnson, D. W., Johnson, R., & Holubec (1987). **Structuring cooperative learning: Lessons plans for teachers**. Edina, MN: Interaction Book Company.

Johnson, D. W., Johnson, R., & Holubec (1988). **Advanced cooperative learning**. Edina, MN: Interaction Book Company.

Johnson, D. W., Johnson, R., & Maruyama G. (1983). Interdependence and interpersonal attraction among heterogeneous and homogeneous individuals: A theoretical formulation and a meta-analysis of the research. **Review of Educational Research, 53,** 5-54.

Johnson, D. W., Johnson, R., & Smith, K. (1986). Academic conflict among students: Controversy and learning. In R. Feldman, (Ed.). **Social psychological applications to education**. Cambridge University Press.

Johnson, D. W., Johnson, R., Stanne, M., & Garibaldi, A. (in press). The impact of leader and member group processing on achievement in cooperative groups. **Journal of Social Psychology.**

Johnson, D. W., Maruyama, G., Johnson, R., Nelson, D., & Skon, L. (1981). Effects of cooperative, competitive, and individualistic goal structures on achievement: A meta-analysis. **Psychological Bulletin, 89,** 47-62.

Johnson, D. W., & Matross, R. (1977). The interpersonal influence of the psychotherapist. In A. Gurman & A. Razin (Eds.), **The effective therapist: A handbook.** Elmsford, NY: Pergamon Press.

Johnson, R. (1976). The relationship between cooperation and inquiry in science classrooms. **Journal of Research in Science Teaching, 10,** 55-63.

Johnson, R., Johnson, D. W. & Bryant, B. (1973). Cooperation and competition in the classroom. **Elementary School Journal, 74,** 172-181.

Kagan, S. (1988). **Cooperative learning: Resources for teachers**. Riverside, California: University of California.

Kerr, N., & Bruun, S. (1981). Ringlemann revisited: Alternative explanations for the social loafing effect. **Personality and Social Psychology Bulletin, 7,** 224-231.

Kohn, A. (1986). **No contest**. Boston: Houghton Mifflin.

Laughlin, P., & McGlynn, R. (1967). Cooperative versus competitive concept attainment as a function of sex and stimulus display. **Journal of Personality and Social Psychology, 7**(4), 398-402.

Latane, B., Williams, K., & Harkins, S. (1975). Many hands make for light work: The causes and consequences of social loafing. **Journal of Personality and Social Psychology, 37,** 822-832.

Lew, M., Mesch, D., Johnson, D. W., & Johnson, R. (1986a). Positive interdependence, academic and collaborative-skills group contingencies and isolated students. **American Educational Research Journal, 23,** 476-488.

Lew, M., Mesch, D., Johnson, D. W., & Johnson, R. (1986b). Components of cooperative learning: Effects of collaborative skills and academic group contingencies on achievement and mainstreaming. **Contemporary Educational Psychology, 11,** 229-239.

Little, J. (1981). **School success and staff development in urban desegregated schools**. Paper presented at the American Educational Research Association, Los Angeles, April.

Male, M., Johnson, R., Johnson, D., & Anderson, M. (1988). **Cooperative learning and computers: An activity guide for teachers**. Santa Cruz, CA: Educational Apple-cations.

Mayer, A. (1903). Uber Einzel-und Gesamtleistung des Schul kindes. **Archiv fur die Gesamte Psychologie, 1,** 276-416.

Mesch, D., Johnson, D. W., & Johnson, R. (1988). Impact of positive interdependence and academic group contingencies in achievement. **Journal of Social Psychology, 128,** 345-352.

Mesch, D., Lew, M., Johnson, D. W., & Johnson, R. (1986). Isolated teenagers, cooperative learning and the training social skills. **Journal of Psychology, 120,** 323-334.

Moede, W. (1920). **Experimentelle massenpsychologie**. Leipzig: S. Hirzel.

Pepitone, E. (1980). **Children in cooperation and competition.** Lexington, MA: Lexington Books.

Petty, R., Harkins, S., Williams, K., & Latane, B. (1977). The effects of group size on cognitive effort and evaluation. **Personality and Social Psychology Bulletin, 3,** 575-578.

Putnam, J., Rynders, J., Johnson, D. W., & Johnson, R. (1989). Collaborative skill instruction for promoting positive interactions between mentally handicapped and nonhandicapped children. **Exceptional Children, 55,** 550-557.

Schumaker, J., Sheldon-Wildgen, J., & Sherman, J. (1980). **An observational study of the academic and social skills of learning disabled adolescents in the regular classroom** (Research Report No. 22). Lawrence, Kansas: University of Kansas Institute for Research in Learning Disabilities.

Sharan, S. (1980). Cooperative learning in teams: Recent methods and effects on achievement, attitudes, and ethnic relations. **Review of Educational Research, 50,** 241-272.

Slavin, R. (1980). Cooperative learning. **Review of Educational Research, 50,** 315-342.

Slavin, R. (1983). **Cooperative learning.** New York: Longman.

Slavin, R., Leavey, M., & Madden, N. (1983). Combining cooperative learning and individual instruction: Effects on student mathematics achievement, attitudes, and behaviors. **Elementary School Journal, 84,** 409-422.

Tjosvold, D. (1986). **Working together to get things done.** Lexington, MA: D. C. Heath.

Tjosvold, D., & Johnson, D. W. (1983). **Productive conflict management.** New York: Irvington.

Triplett, N. (1898). The dynamogenic factors in pacemaking and competition. **American Journal of Psychology, 9,** 507-533.

Watson, G., & Johnson, D. W. (1972). **Social Psychology: Issues and insights.** Philadelphia: Lippincott.

Williams, K. (1981). **The effects of group cohesiveness on social loafing.** Paper presented at the annual meeting of the Midwestern Psychological Association, Detroit.

Williams, K., Harkins, S., & Latane, B. (1981). Identifiability as a deterrent to social loafing: Two cheering experiments. **Journal of Personality and Social Psychology, 40,** 303-311.

Yager, S., Johnson, D. W., & Johnson, R. (1985). Oral discussion, group-to-individual transfer, and achievement in cooperative learning groups. **Journal of Educational Psychology, 77,** 60-66.